Plan Your Gardening Year

ANDREW MIKOLAJSKI

Foreword by Joe Swift

**FLAME TREE
PUBLISHING**

Contents

This is the time when the garden really starts to wake up after winter. With early bulbs making patches of colour and some shrubs starting to flower and providing a foretaste of what's to come later on, you have every incentive to get outdoors and start some important tasks. This season also sees the first of the warm weather, so you won't begrudge the time spent improving the soil for growing your own fruit and vegetables to enjoy later on.

Things really start accelerating now, with more and more flowers opening each day. With damp weather likely, there's usually a rush of growth on perennials, some of which will need staking or can easily be divided to fill beds. You can start off dahlias and lilies for their summer flowers and also begin planning crops such as tomatoes and cucumbers. It is also a good time to sow seeds in the vegetable garden, as most will germinate readily now.

Late Spring

This can be a magical time in the garden with plenty of flowers alongside foliage that is still fresh and green. But beware – warm daytime temperatures can be deceptive at this time of year and sharp frosts can often occur during the night. Be prepared to protect vulnerable plants with fleeces and cloches. With hedging plants making a mass of growth, now is the time to give them their first cut of the year to neaten them for summer.

Early Summer

This time of year usually heralds the start of the rose season, when all the earlier careful pruning and feeding paying off. Clematis and other climbers are lifting your eye skywards as their flowers start to open. It's also the time to prune and tidy up shrubs and trees that have flowered, particularly *Prunus*. Keep a watch out also for certain pests which can now start to proliferate in the warm conditions.

Mid-Summer

Annuals grown from seed fill the garden with colour at this time of year. It's also the season for picking and enjoying many soft fruits. But, as this can also be the hottest time of the year, precious water may be in short supply. You need to pay particular attention to all plants under glass that can suffer under high temperatures.

Avoid a jaded look by giving hedges their second cut and trimming back excessive growth on climbers. A host of beneficial insects are attracted into the garden by the many flowers that should still be opening. You'll be harvesting plums, tomatoes and the first of the apples.

Roses, annuals and late-flowering perennials keep the interest going at this time of year. After a long, hot summer, there is a springlike feel – with the added bonus of more fruit. Now is an good time for lawn maintenance.

Autumn leaf colour is often a highlight of this season as trees and shrubs prepare for winter dormancy. But you'll already be thinking about planting bulbs, sowing seeds and planting out bedding. In the vegetable garden, you'll be harvesting potatoes. This is also a good time for taking cuttings and collecting seed.

With the garden fairly bare now, you can assess to what extent you have created a larder for birds – who will be in need of berries and seeds. You can also give some thought to layout, as this is a good time for moving established shrubs and conifers. You will continue to take cuttings and prepare plants for winter.

Early Winter 224

Why not take some hardwood cuttings? They need minimum aftercare. With frosts likely, it's essential to keep a close watch on vulnerable plants. You also need to keep a close eye on fruits, vegetables and bulbs stored in sheds – they attract mice, which, like the birds, will be foraging for food during milder spells.

Mid-Winter 232

This is an excellent time for taking root cuttings from a number of perennials. Forced hyacinths should now be starting to come into flower indoors. Houseplants – mostly originating in tropical and subtropical regions – can benefit from a light position at this time of year.

Late Winter 240

This can be a busy and exciting season, with early snowdrops and winter aconites. Give overgrown plants a hard prune, remove dead growth from perennials and coax overwintered fuchsias back to life. Start warming up the soil with fleece and cloches in order to plant potatoes and sow seeds earlier.

Foreword

I love gardening and have always found it one of life's pleasures. For me it's all about engaging with the process, tuning into the seasons and, of course, seeing and reaping the rewards of your efforts. It can be hard work at times, but as with many things in life, with gardening you'll get back pretty much what you put in.

I've been at it since I was a kid, starting off gardening with my grandparents and parents, then gardening and designing gardens professionally and now I garden at home with my children, too. I can't get enough

of it and to date haven't found a single down side. It's fun, healthy, creative and relaxing, and, if you grow your own, delicious too! Gardening is also becoming increasingly relevant in the wider view, as we look for sustainable solutions and to provide a diverse range of habitats for wildlife.

To become a really good gardener and develop a special garden, first and foremost it's key to understand the mechanics and practicalities of how a garden works and precisely what to do in each season. Conditioning soil, propagating and growing plants, pruning, looking after the lawn and so on are all skills to be mastered over time.

I have always used gardening books in my career, as having expert knowledge on hand will not only offer inspiration and give confidence, but will also help to avoid too many frustrating mistakes (of course we will all make some and learn quickly from them!).

What to Do When in Your Garden is an excellent, no-nonsense book packed full of solid, simply put and easy-to-follow gardening info and tips. Whether you have a small town courtyard or a large rural garden, it covers an immense amount of ground and will be one of those invaluable books you'll keep going back to for great ideas and advice.

Joe Swift
Garden designer and TV presenter

Introduction

We all admire a beautiful garden but may be baffled as to how to keep one looking good through the year. Is it really necessary to be in the garden from dawn till dusk, have an army of staff or limitless funds – what are the secrets of successful gardening?

Looking Ahead

Experienced gardeners know that maintaining a garden is less a matter of time and money than of forward planning. Gardeners are always thinking about the future. Plant a young shrub and you are already imagining what it will look like when fully grown and covered in flowers; sow some vegetable seeds and in your mind's eye you are sitting down to a delicious meal of home-grown produce.

But most of us have busy lives, with only limited time for gardening, and it's easy to neglect some small task that will actually pay dividends later on. And if you are still new to gardening, you will not have years of experience to fall back on.

If this is the case (or you just need some gentle reminders), keep the following in mind when planning your gardening tasks for the year:

▶ **Soil:** Do you need to prepare the soil for planting either now or in the coming weeks?

▶ **Growing from seed:** Are there any plants you could be raising from seed at this time? If you have seedlings, are they ready for potting on or planting out?

▶ **Cuttings:** Are there any shrubs that you can take cuttings from? Are any cuttings you took a while back now ready for potting on or planting out?

▶ **Planting:** Is now a good time for adding new plants to the garden?

▶ **Lawns:** Is now the best time for making a lawn? If you have a lawn, does it need any attention now, other than mowing?

▶ **Pruning:** Should you be pruning plants at this time of year?

▶ **Under cover:** What should you be doing in the greenhouse to keep plants happy?

▶ **Pests and diseases:** How do you spot the signs of these and what action should you take to deal with them?

▶ **Wildlife:** When should you be taking particular care to protect wildlife?

Spread the Workload

The key to success is to break up the work into easily manageable chunks, so that you can make the best use of your time without having to leave an important job half done. Knowing exactly what needs doing at each particular season in the year will save you wasting valuable time.

Gardening can be a bit like playing the stock market. It's not that everything you do is a gamble, but that, having invested a certain amount of time in a particular task, you may not see the results until some time in the future.

Working With the Seasons

In temperate parts of the globe, we experience four seasons annually, and the typical weather patterns influence plants' growth cycle. It's this annual rhythm in the seasons that determines when is the best time to sow seed, when to prune and when plants may be susceptible to particular pests and diseases.

▶ **Spring:** This season sees an increase in hours of sunlight and warmth. Hard frosts become less frequent (indeed, they may cease altogether in favoured spots). Plants begin to grow rapidly, especially during mild, damp spells, and seeds germinate readily.

▶ **Summer:** A season of long, hot days and shorter nights – at the height of summer in some areas, it scarcely gets dark at all. Many plants open their flowers at this time of year to take advantage of the many pollinating insects that are feeding and looking for mates in the warm weather.

▶ **Autumn:** This time of year can be unpredictable. While there may be a spring-like feel to the weather, with days cooler than summer but still appreciably warm, there's also often a risk of strong gales, which rip fading leaves from trees and shrubs and also help disperse seeds. Lower temperatures persuade many plants to stop growing altogether, even to die back below ground level. They seem to know that winter is on the way.

▶ **Winter:** This is the coldest of the seasons, with short days and long nights, often with freezing temperatures. However, a period of cold is beneficial to hardy plants, as it forces them into dormancy – a state of rest. Many fruit trees and other woody plants that flower early in spring need a certain number of hours at low temperatures. As the weather warms up again in spring, it's as though a switch has been flicked, and they burst into flower.

Understanding the Local Climate

Weather patterns can vary depending on which part of the country you live in. Near the sea, frosts occur much less frequently than inland – the water warms the air slightly. Conversely, the same water cools the air in summer, so it is never quite so hot near the coast as it is inland. Spring seems to arrive much earlier and winters will be shorter. You can always check with the local weather station what the prevailing conditions are in your area.

Equally, weather patterns are never the same from one year to the next, and this too has an impact on plant growth. A period of cold in early spring will delay the flowering of many trees, bulbs and shrubs, which will suddenly all flower at once as the temperature rises.

13

The Hardiness of Plants

Plants are described as hardy if they are capable of surviving freezing temperatures. However, the hardiness of any plant is relative. In areas with reliably long, hot summers, outer tissues toughen and roots penetrate ever deeper in the soil as the upper layer dries out. After so many hours of sunshine, plants are able to survive periods of freezing weather in winter. Conversely, if the summer is cool and damp, plants will make a lot of whippy, leafy growth, which will be very susceptible to frost.

Hence, olive trees – widely grown in parts of the Mediterranean where freezing winters are not unknown – can be considered hardy there because the hot summer sun thickens their bark considerably. In cooler areas, they will need some form of protection to get them through the winter.

Half-hardy and tender plants (including vegetables) cannot survive freezing temperatures, so they can only be grown in the garden during the warmer months – though they can survive short dips below freezing if given the protection of a cloche, cold frame or length of horticultural fleece. If you live near the coast, or other region where frosts seldom occur, by all means take a chance on growing them outside year round.

14

How to Use This Book

The information in this book is presented in twelve chapters, following the months of the year from spring through to winter. Remember that the Northern Hemisphere is the opposite to the Southern Hemisphere, so 'early spring' is March in the Northern Hemisphere or September in the Southern Hemisphere, 'mid-spring' is April or October respectively, 'late spring' is May or November, 'early summer' is June or December, 'mid-summer' is July or January, 'late summer' is August or February, 'early autumn' is September or March, 'mid-autumn' is October or April, 'late autumn' is November or May, 'early winter' is December or June, 'mid-winter' is January or July, and 'late winter' is February or August.

For many gardeners, spring feels like the start of the gardening year, when the soil is workable after the worst winter frosts, spring bulbs are starting to carpet the ground with vivid colour, and many trees and shrubs are flowering on their still leafless stems. Inevitably, there's less to do in winter.

But while most gardening tasks are seasonal, some can be done at various other times, depending on local conditions – and your own timetable. The schedule of tasks outlined in this book is intended as a guide, not a straitjacket. When consulting a particular chapter, it's also worth glancing at the chapters to either side in order to take advantage of periods of unseasonal weather. If it suits you to prune your roses in late winter, go ahead and do so. Plants tend to be forgiving, provided you nurture them correctly.

Each chapter deals first with the ornamental garden, then the indoor garden – whether you have a dedicated greenhouse (heated or not), a conservatory or just a porch or windowsill – and then the kitchen garden.

Early Spring

The Flower Garden

With more daylight hours, you'll want to spend more time outdoors and start to tackle all those jobs you've been thinking about through the winter. You'll see plenty of signs of new life in the garden to keep your motivation level high. The gardener can still be surprised by cold winter snaps at this time of year, however, so try to be cautious and avoid planting or sowing too early.

Beds and Borders

This is the time of year when many people start thinking about their gardens in earnest, as well as what they would like to plant. So, begin improving the soil of bare beds and borders that you are planning to plant later on this season.

Improving the Soil

The simplest way to improve soil is just to fork it over. As you turn over forkloads, you'll be aerating the soil as well as making it easier for excess water to drain through. Remove all large stones, old bits of tree roots and other rubbish you come across – these will impede plant growth. Also pull up all traces of weeds.

What is Soil?

Soil is a mix of clay, silt, sand and humus (decayed bits of old plants and animal remains). In a good garden soil, there'll be a good balance of all of these. Good soil is also teeming with life – earthworms, centipedes and a host of microscopic organisms and fungi.

Lawns

If you have left the lawn unmown over winter, start a regular mowing
regime now.

Making Beds in Lawns

Make beds in lawns to increase the number of plants you
are growing or if you want to plant a specimen tree or shrub. Here are some
ideas for differently shaped beds:

► **Square and oblong beds:** Line up square or rectangular beds with the house
walls or a garden path – not the boundaries of the garden, which are often not
true. Use a builder's square to ensure the angles are correct.

► **Round beds:** Drive a stake or cane into the ground where you want the
centre of the bed to be. Attach a length of string to this, then measure off
and mark on it the radius of the circle. Pull the string taut and grasp
the mark. With a can of spray paint in your hand, run round the stake,
spraying the grass to mark the circle.

► **Oval beds:** To create an oval shape, mark two overlapping circles of
differing sizes as described above. Run a garden hose around the two
circles and use this as a guide when cutting the oval shape.

► **Kidney-shaped beds:** Use a length of garden hose or rope to mark the
outline of the bed. Hold this in position with tent pegs or stout lengths of
wire, and then cut out the shape.

Top Tip

When cutting
shapes in lawns,
use a half-moon
cutter rather than
a spade, which will
not cut straight lines.

Laying Turf

Turf provides an instant solution if you want to make a new lawn.

▶ **Establish a shape:** Mark out the area of the new lawn.

▶ **Prepare the ground:** Dig over the soil, removing all large stones and traces of perennial weeds. Lightly tread the soil to consolidate the surface, and then rake it level.

▶ **Start to lay:** Lay the first strip of turf along one of the edges. Cut to size with a sharp knife.

▶ **Use a plank:** Lay a plank on the strip you have just laid, using this to spread your weight as you lay the second and subsequent rows.

▶ **Tidy up:** Tamp down each strip of turf with the back of a rake.

▶ **Water in:** Keep the new lawn well watered for the first six months after laying.

Top Tip
When mowing the lawn, give only a light trim initially if the grass is high. You can make a closer cut the following week.

Top Tip
When laying turf, be sure to butt all the joins tightly together so that the turfs knit well.

Wildlife

Many mammals will be starting to emerge from hibernation and birds will be returning home to begin nesting. Insects will start hunting for pollen on dry, sunny days.

Wildlife Hedges

Prune wildlife hedges early, before the birds have started nesting. Be careful not to remove flower-bearing stems (flower buds should be beginning to swell), as these are important for bees and other pollinating insects. Cut back completely any vigorous, overlong branches that are not flower-bearing.

Early Flowers for Wildlife

Aubrieta

Crocus

Daphne

Helleborus (hellebores)

Muscari (grape hyacinth)

Primula veris (cowslip)

Scilla (squill)

Skimmia

Tulipa (tulip)

Viola labradorica

(Alpine violet)

Birds

Stop putting food out for birds – they should be finding their own food sources now. Make sure that bird boxes are securely attached to trees and house walls and that they are out of reach of cats.

Frogs and Toads

Frogs and toads often shelter in long grass or among piles of stones or bricks. If you are planning a general tidy-up in the garden, leave such areas undisturbed if these amphibians are frequent visitors to your garden. Wait until later in the season when they are active.

Pollinating Insects

Flighted insects will be active on warm days. Make sure you have plenty of early flowers to attract them. Not only are pollinating insects important to the ecology of the garden overall, but many help in controlling the numbers of pests.

Trees and Shrubs

This is a good time of year for planting new evergreen trees and shrubs such as hollies, camellias and ceanothus. To plant a container-grown tree or shrub:

▶ **Dig a hole:** Make sure that the hole is slightly larger than the container you have bought the plant in.

▶ **Prepare the hole:** Loosen the soil at the base of the hole with a hand fork.

▶ **Line the hole:** Line the base of the hole with garden compost or other soil improver.

▶ **Plant:** Slide the plant from the container and place it in the centre of the hole – the top of the compost should be level with the surrounding soil.

▶ **Fill in:** With a trowel, fill in the gap around the roots with the excavated soil mixed with garden compost or soil improver.

▶ **Firm in:** Lightly firm in the plant with your hands – not too much, or you may compact the soil surface.

▶ **Water:** Water the plant well.

Rhododendrons and Azaleas

These beautiful shrubs are appearing in garden centres now, most producing their trumpet-like flowers during the spring. Many are evergreen and the flowers can be scented. Flower colours include white, pink, red, yellow, orange and purple. A few key points to bear in mind when growing this group of plants are as follows:

▶ **Container plants:** These glamorous plants thrive in tubs and containers and look good next to the front door – but you must use ericaceous compost, which has been specially formulated for these plants.

▶ **Sun or shade:** Most prefer a shaded site, but not deep shade. Dwarf rhododendrons are alpine plants that will take full sun.

Did You Know?

Ever been puzzled by the difference between rhododendrons and azaleas? Actually – there isn't one!

23

Pruning

Prune shrubs that have already flowered. Cut back older stems that are bare at the base to ground level. Thin the remaining stems to create an open, vase-shaped plant, and then shorten stems that have flowered by up to one third (you may leave some stems unpruned).

Top Tip

If you live in a cold area, delay pruning fuchsias until mid-spring.

Coppicing

Some plants are grown for their colourful winter stems. These should be cut hard back now to a low, woody framework of stems up to 10 cm (6 in) high. Hard pruning can encourage other plants to produce larger leaves than normal and also keeps them within bounds. Prune hardy fuchsias, the butterfly bush (*Buddleja davidii*), Russian sage (*Perovskia*) and *Hydrangea paniculata* in the same way.

After pruning, feed, water and mulch the plant well to encourage the plant to recover and produce new growth.

Trees and Shrubs for Coppicing

Berberis	leaves
Catalpa bignonioides	leaves
Cornus (dogwood)	stems
Cotinus (smoke bush)	leaves
Eucalyptus	leaves
Paulownia tomentosa	leaves
Rubus thibetanus	stems
Salix (willow)	stems

Growing Roses

Roses should just be showing signs of new life, with green buds breaking all along the stems.

Bush Roses

Roses can vary in size. Choose the right type of rose for the space you have available:

- ▶ **Shrub roses:** Large plants, up to 2 m (6 ft) high or more. They make good specimens.

- ▶ **Floribunda roses:** These are smaller than shrub roses, with clusters of flowers over a long period.

- ▶ **Hybrid teas:** These have larger flowers that are suitable for cutting.

- ▶ **Patio roses:** More compact, with clusters of small flowers that are sometimes followed by bright red hips.

- ▶ **Ground-cover roses:** Similar to patio roses, but are low-growing and spreading.

- ▶ **Miniature roses:** These are only 30 cm (12 in) tall or less. They are excellent for a dwarf hedge.

25

Standard Roses

Standard roses ('rose trees') are created artificially by grafting a rose bush at the top of a tall stem. They are always top-heavy, so must be sited in a part of the garden sheltered from strong winds. They should also be staked on planting (*see* 'Staking Perennials', p. 44).

Planting a Rose

Now is probably your last chance to buy and plant bare-root roses (see p. 182). To plant a container-grown rose, *see* 'Trees and Shrubs' (p. 22).

General Care

Give established roses their first feed of the season. A fertilizer specially formulated for roses is best – these have the correct balance of plant nutrients to ensure good flowering and general health. Remember to:

▶ Fork the fertilizer around the base of each bush.

▶ Apply the product at the rate specified by the manufacturer – giving too much feed can be counter-productive and may harm the plant.

▶ Water well after feeding and mulch to conserve soil moisture.

Top Tip

If you are pruning a number of rose bushes, clean your secateurs carefully after you have finished each one. This prevents the possible spread of disease from one rose to another.

Pruning an Established Rose

If you are pruning a rose that is already established, remember to:

▶ Cut back all dead, diseased and damaged stems.

▶ Cut back all weak, twiggy growth.

▶ Shorten the remaining stems by up to a half, cutting back to an outward-facing bud.

▶ Feed, water and mulch.

Planting New Perennials

Providing the ground is not waterlogged or frozen, early spring is one of the best times to plant new perennials, as follows:

▶ **Prepare the ground:** Dig over the soil, removing any perennial weeds such as couch grass and bindweed.

▶ **Feed the soil:** Fork in plenty of garden compost, well-rotted farmyard manure or soil improver and add a handful of general fertilizer.

▶ **Plant:** Dig a hole twice the width of the new plant's container. Slide the plant out of the container, set it in the middle of the hole, then backfill with the excavated soil.

▶ **Water:** Firm in the plant with your hands, then water thoroughly.

Dividing Snowdrops

Most snowdrops have finished flowering by now, and this is the best time either to move them or to divide congested clumps – while they are still in leaf. Simply fork up the clumps and separate the bulbs. Replant in their new positions. Do not be alarmed if the foliage collapses after replanting. The leaves are dying back anyway, and the bulbs will flower again next winter.

Sowing Hardy Annuals

Seeds of hardy annuals, such as poached-egg plant (*Limnanthes douglasii*) and love-in-a-mist (*Nigella damascena*), can be sown in the open ground where they are to flower.

▶ **Sow:** Weed the ground and rake it level, then sow the seed either in rows or by scattering it. (Sowing in rows makes it easier to distinguish the emerging seedlings from weeds.)

▶ **Soil:** Cover the seeds lightly with sieved soil. Water in dry weather.

▶ **Thin:** When the seedlings are large enough to handle, thin them to the distances recommended on the seed packet.

Planting out Sweet Peas

If you sowed sweet peas (*Lathyrus odoratus*) in autumn, they can be planted out in their flowering positions now.

Supporting the Plants

Sweet peas are climbers that need a support for the stems to cling to. To support your sweet peas as they grow, you will need:

▶ **Walls and fences:** Pin lengths of chicken wire or pig wire against walls and fences.

▶ **Beds and borders:** Use pea sticks (whippy hazel branches sold in bundles) stuck in the ground or make wigwams of lengths of bamboo or cane. Alternatively, wrap a length of chicken wire around four or five stakes driven into the ground.

▶ **Formal gardens:** For a more formal effect, use a ready-made obelisk or arch.

▶ **Kitchen gardens:** To provide cut flowers, use crossed poles tied to a horizontal, as for runner beans (see p. 79).

Top Tip

Keep all new plantings well watered until they are established.

29

Gardening Under Cover

Not only is there much to do outdoors, but you can also get cracking inside. Even if you don't have a greenhouse or conservatory, you can make use of kitchen windowsills and spare bedrooms.

Sowing Seed

You can steal a march by raising new plants from seed – both for the flower garden and vegetables – under cover, before the weather has really warmed up. If you don't have a greenhouse, a bright windowsill can be just as useful.

Propagators

You can speed up the germination of seeds by using a propagator. Simple models comprise a seed tray and a fitting clear plastic cover with vents that can be opened and closed. More sophisticated models have a heat cable in the base. Larger propagators often have thermostatic controls. Whatever type you use, open and close the vents to regulate the temperature and raise or lower humidity around the seedlings.

Houseplants

Many houseplants can look a bit tatty by the end of winter. Refresh them as follows:

▶ **Tidy up:** Remove any dead leaves.

▶ **Clean:** Gently wipe the leaves with a damp cloth.

▶ **Refresh:** Scrape away the compost at the top of the pot and replace with fresh.

▶ **Spray:** Mist the plants, especially if they are in centrally heated rooms.

▶ **Water:** Water them more frequently.

▶ **Feed:** Apply a special houseplant feed to give an instant boost.

Top Tip

If begonia tubers are very large and you can see several growth buds, cut them up into sections, each with at least one bud. Dust the cut surfaces with a fungicidal powder.

Begonias

Begonia tubers

If you have stored some begonia tubers over winter, coax them back into life for use in summer containers and hanging baskets.

▶ **Prepare a tray:** Fill a tray with some potting compost and dampen this thoroughly. Allow the water to drain away.

▶ **Position carefully:** Place the tubers on the compost surface. The concave surface of the tuber should be facing upwards. Lightly press them into the compost.

▶ **Store well:** Keep the trays in good light (but out of direct sunlight) and at a temperature of around 20°C (68°F).

▶ **Feed:** When the new shoots are growing strongly, feed with a tomato fertilizer at half strength.

Amaryllis

Amaryllis (or *Hippeastrum*) bulbs will probably
have finished flowering by now. Rather than
discarding them, you can build up the bulb for
replanting next winter. You will need to do
the following in order to achieve this:

▶ **Flowers:** Remove the faded
flowers where they meet the stem
at the top. (Leave the stem to die
back naturally.)

▶ **Light:** Keep the plant in good light.

▶ **Water and food:** Water frequently and feed
weekly with a tomato fertilizer at
half strength.

▶ **Leaves:** When the foliage begins to turn yellow, stop
watering and feeding. Allow the foliage to die back
completely. When the leaves are completely dry and
withered, pull them away from the neck of the bulb.

▶ **Storage:** Store the dry bulb in a cool, dry place (such
as a spare bedroom).

The Kitchen Garden

With most of the soil improvement done over winter, you can now set to and start planting. All the work you do now will be amply repaid when you harvest your crops later.

Improving the Soil

For growing productive crops, the ground has to be fertile and well drained. Adding garden compost or well-rotted animal manures to the soil before planting guarantees good results.

To raise the nutrient level of the soil, you can also fork in a general garden fertilizer that will break down slowly over the year as the plants are growing. Pelleted chicken manure is a popular organic fertilizer. Always apply fertilizers at the rate recommended by the manufacturer.

Soil Additives

Horse manure is excellent for adding bulk to light soils. It does not contain many plant nutrients and may contain weed seeds.

Poultry manure is high in uric acid and can scorch plants if allowed to touch them. Use with caution or (better) as an activator in a compost heap.

Spent mushroom compost usually contains chalk, so is unsuitable for use on soils that are already very alkaline.

Note: Animal manures should be stacked for six to twelve months before use. Correctly rotted down, they are odour-free and pleasant to handle.

Raised Beds

Many gardeners use raised beds, usually 15–20 cm (6–8 in) deep, for growing vegetables. Farmyard manure and/or garden compost can simply be heaped into these a few weeks before planting. The beds can be made very simply by cutting railway sleepers to the desired length or by nailing planks of wood to short stakes driven into the soil.

Parsnips

This popular root vegetable can be sown in the open ground, in well-prepared soil. Sow the seed thinly, around 15 cm (6 in) apart in shallow drills.

Note: At low temperatures, germination can be slow so, if you live in a cold area, delay planting till later in the season. Alternatively, plant seeds individually in modules under cover for planting out later.

Onions

Unlike most other vegetables, onions and shallots are not grown from seed but from 'sets' – small individual bulbs. Simply push these into well-prepared ground with the tips slightly protruding.

Peaches

Peach trees flower early in the year, before many pollinating insects are active. To ensure good fruiting, it's best to pollinate the flowers yourself. Choose a dry sunny day when the flowers are open. Dab the tip of a small paintbrush on the stamens of each

Sowing shallots

flower to collect the yellow pollen grains. Brush the pollen onto another flower's stigma, which you'll find in the centre of each.

Peach Leaf Curl

Peaches are notoriously prone to a condition known as peach leaf curl, caused by the fungus *Taphrina deformans*. The leaves pucker and blister on the branch. Fortunately, this is not life-threatening. Simply pick off all affected leaves and burn them (do not compost them).

Trees usually recover well. Feed and water well, and new leaves that are unaffected will soon appear.

35

Plants To Enjoy

Trees

Acacia

Cupressus macrocarpa
  'Goldcrest'

Magnolia x soulangeana

Shrubs

Camellia

Chaenomeles (ornamental
  quince, japonica)

Corylopsis

Forsythia

Corylus (hazel)

Daphne mezereum

Euphorbia

Forsythia

Hamamelis (witch hazel)

Lonicera fragrantissima

Magnolia stellata
  (star magnolia)

Mahonia

Pieris

Ribes (flowering currant)

Salix (willow)

Spiraea thunbergii

Climbers

Clematis alpina

Clematis macropetala

Perennials

Bergenia (elephant's ears)

Helleborus (hellebore)

Bulbs

Chionodoxa
  (glory of the snow)

Crocus

Eranthis (winter aconite)

Erythronium
  (dog's tooth violet)

Galanthus (snowdrop)

Hyacinthus (hyacinth)

Iris danfordiae

Muscari (grape hyacinth)

Narcissus (daffodil)

Scilla (squill)

Tulipa kaufmanniana

Annuals and biennials

Primula, Polyanthus Group
  (polyanthus)

Bellis perennis (daisy)

Viola, Wittrockiana Group
  (pansy)

Checklist

▶ **Soil:** Improve the soil by adding an improver – garden compost, well-rotted farmyard manure or in bags from the garden centre. This is especially important in the vegetable garden.

▶ **Lawns:** Start a regular mowing regime now that the grass is starting to perk up again. Make new lawns using turf.

▶ **Snowdrops:** Divide congested clumps, especially if flowering has been disappointing this year.

▶ **Seeds:** Sow seeds of flowers and vegetables for the summer. Keep these under cover if the weather stays cold. Hardy annuals can be sown outside, either in a nursery bed or in their intended positions.

▶ **Sweet peas:** Plant out seedlings or sow some seed now. Make supports for the plants.

▶ **Roses:** Prune roses, which should be shooting strongly. Feed well with a rose fertilizer, then water and mulch around the base of each plant.

▶ **Houseplants:** Freshen up houseplants by removing dead foliage, wiping over leaves and increasing how often you water them. Many will also benefit from feeding.

▶ **Vegetables:** Sow the seed of vegetables that need a long growing season. Plant onion sets.

▶ **Peaches:** Hand-pollinate peaches, especially if they are growing against a wall. Remove all leaves that show signs of peach leaf curl.

Mid-Spring

The Flower Garden

The garden begins to fill with colour as the weather warms up, with many spring shrubs and bulbs in flower. Mid-spring is a great time for moving and dividing plants in readiness for the main summer display.

Lawns

You can create a new lawn using either turf or seed. A significant advantage of seed, however, is that you have much more choice over the type of lawn you'll end up with. For example, you can buy seed mixes for a fine sward, for a lawn that will stand up to hard use (if you have children and dogs), or for a shady site.

Sowing a Lawn

A new area of grass can be created with seed and is a cheaper, though slower, option than laying turf (see p. 20), as follows:

▶ **Soil:** Dig over the site, clearing it of all weeds and large stones. Break down any large clods. If the soil is poor, add organic matter or soil improver and grit for good drainage. Firm the soil and then rake it level.

▶ **Sow:** Scatter the seed at the recommended rate for the variety. Lightly rake over the surface.

▶ **Water:** If the weather continues dry, keep the site well watered until the seed germinates.

▶ **Roll:** Once the blades are 5 cm (2 in) in height, roller the seedlings to consolidate the roots. (This means you won't pull them from the ground the first time you mow.)

▶ **Mow:** A few days later, give the grass a light trim with the mower.

Note: If germination appears patchy, the seed was probably sown unevenly. Re-sow any bare patches and, as far as practical, thin overcrowded blades.

General Lawn Care

Carry on mowing established lawns. For good growth, apply a nitrogen-high lawn feed to the grass to encourage lush growth. Products containing iron (Fe) will make the grass look darker. If you have clumps of spring bulbs such as crocuses or daffodils (Narcissus) in the grass, mow round the clumps so that the bulb leaves can die back naturally – important for future flowering.

Synthetic Lawns

On a roof garden, or any other situation where grass either won't grow or would be difficult to maintain, you could try an artificial lawn made of a synthetic material. These are not entirely maintenance free, however – they will need regular brushing and hosing to keep them looking good.

41

Planting an Evergreen Hedge

Unlike deciduous hedging plants (see p. 67), evergreen hedge plants are usually sold in containers. Plants for dwarf hedges, such as box (*Buxus*) and lavender (*Lavandula*), are often available in small modules, like bedding plants. Some nurseries specialize in hedging plants.

Improve the soil before planting, as for trees and shrubs (see p. 33). Dig holes of the appropriate size for each plant at the recommended planting distance – usually 60–90 cm (2–3 ft) between each plant. Plants for dwarf hedges can be planted more tightly.

Note: For a denser hedge, plant a double, staggered row, with up to 45 cm (18 in) between them.

Hedging

Evergreen hedging plants

Berberis darwinii

Cotoneaster lacteus

x Cupressocyparis leylandii (Leylandii conifer)

Elaeagnus x ebbingei

Escallonia

Ilex aquifolium (holly)

Prunus laurocerasus (cherry laurel)

Taxus baccata (yew)

Thuja plicata (Western red cedar)

Dwarf hedging plants

Buxus (box)

Lavandula (lavender)

Lonicera nitida

Rosmarinus (rosemary)

Rosmarinus (rosemary)

The Dreaded Leylandii Conifers

Leylandii conifers have had a bad press. If you want a quick-growing evergreen hedge, they are the obvious choice. But they need regular cuts – at least four a year – to keep them in bounds.

Shrubs in Containers

If you have any shrubs in large containers, they will now start to grow strongly. Start watering and feeding them regularly. It's necessary to water even after a shower of rain, as the leaf canopy will probably prevent rain from hitting the compost surface – particularly if the shrub is positioned next to a house wall.

Repotting and Top-Dressing

If the plant has reached the desired size, but has been in the container for several years, you can refresh it by repotting it, as follows:

▶ **Clean:** Carefully remove the plant and scrape away all the old compost from around the roots with your fingers. You may find it easier to wash away the compost with a strong jet of water from a garden hose.

▶ **Cut back:** Trim back the roots by up to one third with secateurs.

43

▶ **Repot:** Wash the pot thoroughly, and then return the plant to it, using fresh compost.

▶ **Top-dress:** If the plant is too large to repot, top-dress it instead. Tilt the pot and, with your fingers, scrape away as much of the upper layer of compost as you can. Replace this with fresh potting compost.

▶ **Feed:** After repotting or top-dressing, add fertilizer pellets that will feed the plant throughout the coming growing season.

Perennials

Most perennials flower in late spring and summer, and will be making good growth now. Some will benefit from a bit of extra attention now if they are to look their best later on.

Staking Perennials

Certain perennials with large flowers need staking, or the weight of the flowers can make the stems collapse. It's best to stake the plants while they are still at an early stage of development. You can use different methods of support:

▶ **Canes:** Drive canes into the soil behind tall perennials such as delphiniums and verbascums. Tie the stems loosely to the stake as they lengthen.

Verbascum

▶ **Ring stakes:** Use ring stakes for clump-forming peonies (*Paeonia*). These comprise a mesh disc, through which the stems grow, supported on uprights. The disc can be raised on the uprights as the stems lengthen.

▶ **Other methods:** You can also make supports for plants by pushing in twiggy pea sticks among them or by wrapping lengths of chicken wire around canes or short lengths of bamboo.

Dividing Perennials

Clump-forming perennials such as hardy geraniums, astrantias and daylilies (*Hemerocallis*) can be dug up and divided. This eases congestion in the plant, as well as giving you plenty of new material for planting elsewhere. This technique also enables you to eliminate older portions of the plant that may have become woody – asters and other plants with daisy flowers tend to do this.

Hemerocallis (daylily)

▶ **Prepare:** Dig up clumps with a fork. Shake the roots free of excess soil.

▶ **Propagate:** Divide the plant into smaller pieces, either with your hands or a hand fork. To split a large clump, use two forks back to back.

▶ **Discard:** Get rid of older, unproductive sections.

▶ **New plants:** Replant the sections, either in the same place or in another part of the garden, firm them in with your hands, and then water well.

▶ **Water:** Water the divisions daily over the next few weeks if the weather is dry.

Dahlias

In mild areas, dahlia tubers can be planted out in the garden, either in borders or in the kitchen garden to provide cut flowers. If late frosts are likely where you garden, start off the tubers in containers in a sheltered position outdoors, in a cold frame, porch or unheated greenhouse.

Planting Dahlias

Plant out dahlia tubers in late spring or early summer, as follows:

▶ **Prepare:** For planting bare tubers, dig holes large enough to accommodate each one.

▶ **Plant and stake:** As you position the tuber, insert a slim cane, around 1.1 m (4 ft) long – or more or less, depending on the predicted height of the variety – next to the main stem, driving this far enough into the ground to keep it stable. Feed in soil around the tuber. Holding it by the stem, shake the tuber gently as you do so to settle the soil around it and eliminate air pockets.

Top Tip

To divide a congested hosta, dig up the clump and then cut it into sections with a sharp knife, just as you would cut a cake into pieces for sharing.

Dahlia tuber

▶ **Water:** Water the tubers in well, and then water them daily if the weather is dry.

▶ **Tie in:** Attach the stems to the canes as they grow.

Top Tip

As lilies appreciate good dranage, replace up to one third of the compost with horticultural grit or sand well mixed in.

▶ **Feed:** For the best flowering, the tubers will benefit from regular feeding. Use a tomato fertilizer or similar product formulated to promote flowering. These are best applied as a root drench at weekly or fortnightly intervals.

Lilies in Pots

Lily bulbs are available now, often sold alongside dahlias. As they need deep planting and are very fussy about good drainage, it is easiest to grow them in pots. Check whether the variety you have chosen need acid soil – if so, you will have to use an ericaceous compost. Select a large pot, at least 30 cm (12 in) deep. Line the base with crocks or chunks of polystyrene, then top with a 5 cm (2 in) layer of potting compost. Place the bulbs on this, then fill the remainder with compost. Top with a layer of grit.

Off With Their Heads

Removing the faded flowers ('dead-heading') of daffodils (*Narcissus*) diverts the plant's energies away from seed production and into building up the bulb – vital for next year's flowers.

Ponds

Ponds are often neglected over winter. Top up the water if the level has dropped over the winter. Thin oxygenating plants as necessary. Frogs and toads will start to spawn at this time of year.

Dividing a Waterlily

It's easiest to divide waterlilies now, just before they start growing strongly, as follows:

▶ **Prepare:** Lift the waterlily rhizome from the base of the pond. Under running water, wash off all the mud from the tuber. Trim back any overlong roots with secateurs and cut off any damaged leaves.

▶ **Divide:** Cut the rhizome into pieces, making sure each section has roots and leaves (or leaf buds).

▶ **Pot up:** Pot up the sections in aquatic baskets using ordinary garden soil. Top with grit and large stones, and then return the sections to the pond.

Slugs and Snails

These molluscs are among the worst of all garden pests. They will attack the soft young growth of many border plants (especially hostas, dahlias and delphiniums) and all seedlings.

They are active from mid-spring onwards, especially during damp weather. There are various methods of control:

▶ Spread poisonous pellets around the plants.

▶ Make collars for individual plants from slug-repellent fabrics.

▶ Run copper tape around the rims of plants in containers.

▶ Use the parasitic nematode, watered in around plants from mid-spring onwards (effective onlyon slugs).

Note: Parasitic nematodes are only sold via mail order by specialist suppliers.

Be an Eco-Warrior

Some gardeners are uncomfortable with the idea of using chemical controls, preferring to patrol the garden at night with a torch, picking off slugs and snails by hand. Dispose of them according to your conscience.

Gardening Under Cover

With night frosts still likely in many areas, you'll need to take full advantage of whatever space you can spare in the house, conservatory or greenhouse for plants you can put outside in early summer.

Sowing Tender Vegetables

Some popular vegetables, such as marrows, courgettes and outdoor cucumbers, are not hardy but still need to be sown now if they are to crop in summer. To sow tender vegetables in pots:

▶ **Prepare:** Fill small pots with seed compost (or multi-purpose compost) to within about 1 cm (½ in) of the rim. Water well and allow to drain.

▶ **Seed:** Sow the seeds on the compost surface and then cover with a light sprinkling of compost. Keep them at a temperature of around 18°C (65°F).

▶ **Plant:** Grow on the seedlings under cover until all risk of frost has passed, when they can be planted outdoors.

50

Pots, Trays and Modules

If you are starting seed off under cover, you need to decide which type of container to use. Choose from the following options:

Small pots are suitable for large seed that can be spaced evenly on the compost. If you use a 12.5 cm (5 in) pot, the seedlings can stay in the container until they are large enough for transplanting into their final positions.

Trays are ideal for very fine seed that is difficult to sow individually.

Modules are useful for seeds large enough to sow individually but that you want to transplant at an early stage in their development. It's also easy to judge when the little plants need planting out or moving to larger containers – when the roots fill the module.

Tomatoes

Tomatoes are one of the most rewarding crops. The plants produce fruits (and a tomato is technically a fruit) over a long period, and the flavour is far superior to anything you can buy in the shops.

Sowing Tomatoes

You can start tomatoes off from seed under cover, as follows:

▶ **Prepare:** Fill seed trays or modules with potting or seed compost, water well and allow to drain.

▶ **Sow:** Lightly press the seeds onto the compost surface, then sprinkle a thin layer of compost over, just to cover them.

▶ **Warmth:** Keep the seeds in a warm position – around 20°C (68°F) – in good light (but not direct sunlight, which can scorch the emerging seedlings).

▶ **Pot on:** Pot up the seedlings individually when they have two or three leaves, then grow them on in cooler conditions.

Did You Know?

Tomatoes are always grown in large containers in fresh potting compost or in growbags, because they are very susceptible to diseases in the soil. This applies both to outdoor and greenhouse varieties.

Houseplants

To revive tired-looking houseplants, place them outdoors during wet weather, in a sheltered position. The rain will soon refresh them, but check the undersides of the pots carefully before you bring them in – you may find small slugs sheltering there.

The Kitchen Garden

Between now and the end of spring is one of the busiest times in the kitchen garden. Not only can you start to move seedlings you've raised indoors into their final positions, but you can also start sowing outside – particularly if there is no risk of a late frost.

Preparing a Seed Bed

Rake a seed bed thoroughly just before planting. Break up any clods of soil with the back of the rake. Pull up any weed seedlings.

How to Sow Seed

How you sow seed in open ground depends on the size of the seed and your dexterity.

Whichever type of crop you are growing, make shallow drills in the soil with a draw hoe, or press the long handle of a rake into the soil to make an indentation.

▶ **Prepare:** Water the drills before sowing the seed to ensure good adhesion between the seed and the soil.

▶ **Large seed:** Sow large seeds (for instance, of peas and beans) individually at the distance recommended on the packet – a technique known as 'station sowing'. Some seed germinates erratically. Station sow three or four seeds together.

53

Top Tip

To save time, look out for seed tapes. These are tapes that have the seeds embedded within them at the recommended distance between each one and can simply be laid in the drill. The tapes break down in the soil.

Sweetcorn From Seed

Sweetcorn is easily raised from seed but needs a slightly different treatment to most other crops. Rather than sowing in rows, the plants should be in blocks to ensure good pollination between the plants. Plant the seeds in groups of four or more for the best results.

▶ **Thin:** When the seedlings emerge, pull up and discard the weaker ones.

▶ **Fine seed:** Very fine seed – for instance, that of lettuce and other salad crops – should be sprinkled lightly along the drill. Thin them to the recommended distance when large enough to handle.

▶ **Soil:** Draw the surrounding soil lightly over the seed with a rake and then water well.

Protecting Crops

Birds often pull up young crops if these are not protected. The simplest way is to drive stakes or canes around the crops and stretch a length of netting over. Secure the netting all around the sides with tent pegs or large stones or bricks. If the mesh is fine, this is also an excellent method of keeping off flighted insect pests that are looking to lay their eggs on plants that will feed their larvae. Alternatively, simply spread a sheet of horticultural fleece over the crops, securing it along the edges with large stones. (This is also a very effective method of protecting young crops from hard frosts on cold nights.) Raise the fleece as the crops grow.

Potatoes

Potatoes are not grown from seed
but from small potatoes (confusingly referred to
as 'seed potatoes'). Potatoes are not fully hardy,
so early plantings usually need some kind of
protection in cold districts.

Chitting

For early crops from the tubers, get
them growing indoors before you plant them in the
garden – a process known as 'chitting'. Inspect
the tubers closely, and you should be able to
identify small sprouts or 'eyes'. Put the tubers on
a tray (such as is used for eggs) with most of the
eyes on each tuber facing upwards. Keep them in
a light position indoors or near a shed or garage
window. Plant the tubers out when the shoots are
no more than 2.5 cm (1 in) long.

Planting

Plant the tubers about 40 cm
(15 in) apart, digging a hole for each one
up to 15 cm (6 in) deep. Plant them with the
eyes (or shoots, if you have chitted them)
facing upwards.

Early Potatoes

If you live in a cold area but want early potatoes, you will need to protect the tubers by spreading a sheet of thick black plastic over them. Cut crosses in the plastic for the stems to grow through. Potato foliage that collapses as a result of frost usually perks up when the weather turns mild again.

Top Tip

If you garden in a cold area, warm up the soil by covering it with a cloche or sheet of horticultural fleece or thick black plastic for two weeks before planting potatoes.

Asparagus

Unlike most other vegetable crops, which are raised annually from fresh seed, asparagus is a perennial that provides a crop every year. It's a crop for the longer term – the plants need to establish for a year or two before you can pick the spears. While it is possible to grow the plants from seed, you'll get more reliable results by planting asparagus 'crowns' in spring.

Making an Asparagus Bed

Dig a trench in well-prepared ground, around 30 cm (12 in) across and 10 cm (4 in) deep. Space the asparagus crowns about 40 cm (16 in) apart in the trench, then cover with soil. Keep them well watered while they are in active growth.

56

Harvesting

Harvest the asparagus spears over a six- to eight-week period in mid-spring. With a sharp knife, cut them from the crown just below soil level.

Top Tip

In order not to exhaust the young asparagus plants, cut only a few spears the first year after planting. The following year, cut the spears only over four weeks.

Protecting Fruit Blossom

Flowers on fruit trees are very susceptible to frost. A cold night can ruin this season's crop, so you need to be vigilant. Wrap lengths of horticultural fleece around the top-growth of vulnerable plants in the evening. You can attach this to stems with clothes pegs. If you don't have fleece, sheets of newspaper can be just as effective. Remove all coverings the following morning. It's not usually practical to protect the blossom on a very large tree.

Pests and Diseases

This is the time of year when you will need to start being vigilant over pests and diseases in the kitchen garden. Be on the lookout for slugs and snails, aphids and birds.

Slugs and Snails

Slugs and snails become a problem at this time of year. For reliable methods of control, see p. 49.

Birds

Birds peck at flower buds and can pull crops from the ground. Protect young vegetables with netting. If you are growing a large number of fruiting plants, invest in a dedicated fruit cage. Netting large trees is not recommended – birds are easily trapped in the mesh.

Aphids

Aphids is a generic term for a large number of common insect pests – including greenfly and blackfly – that suck the sap from plant stems and leaves. They are usually easy to control, either with an insecticide or, more simply, a jet of water from a garden hose. Deal with them as soon as you see them, before they have a chance to breed. Spray the undersides of leaves as well as the upper surfaces.

Plants To Enjoy

Trees

Acacia

Amelanchier

Magnolia x soulangeana

Malus (crab apple)

Prunus (ornamental cherry)

Malus (crab apple)

Shrubs

Camellia

Chaenomeles (ornamental quince, *japonica*)

Coronilla

Cytisus praecox (broom)

Euphorbia

Forsythia

Fothergilla

Kerria

Lavandula (lavender)

Magnolia stellata

Mahonia

Osmanthus

Photinia

Pieris

Rhododendron

Rosmarinus (rosemary)

Ribes (flowering currant)

Viburnum

Magnolia

Chaenomeles (ornamental quince)

59

Climbers

Actinidia kolomikta

Clematis armandii

Perennials

Aubrieta

Bergenia (elephant's ears)

Caltha palustris
   (kingcup, marsh marigold)

Convallaria (lily-of-the-valley)

Dicentra (bleeding heart)

Doronicum

Hosta

Primula

Pulmonaria (lungwort)

Pulsatilla vulgaris (Pasque flower)

Bulbs

Anemone blanda

Erythronium (dog's tooth violet)

Fritillaria (fritillary)

Hyacinthus (hyacinth)

Leucojum (snowflake)

Muscari (grape hyacinth)

Narcissus (daffodil)

Scilla (squill)

Tulipa (tulip)

Annuals and biennials

Lunaria annua (honesty)

Dicentra (bleeding heart)

60

Checklist

▶ **Lawns:** Make new lawns from seed. Feed established lawns with a lawn fertilizer.

▶ **Hedges:** Plant evergreen hedges. Feed all new hedges (up to one year old).

▶ **Shrubs in containers:** Start watering plants regularly and give them a dose of an appropriate fertilizer. Pot on or repot shrubs that have filled their containers.

▶ **Perennials:** Stake perennials with tall or weak stems, either with short canes, plant supports or pea sticks. Dig up and divide congested clumps so that they will flower well later on.

▶ **Bulbs in the garden:** Dead-head all bulbs that have flowered in order to build up the bulbs for next year.

▶ **Dahlias:** Start tubers into growth, either in the garden or in pots for planting out in warmer weather.

▶ **Lilies:** Plant lily bulbs in large containers filled with a free-draining potting compost.

▶ **Vegetables:** Sow seed of a range of vegetables. Tender ones should be started off in warm conditions indoors. Others can be sown in drills made in prepared soil outdoors.

▶ **Crop protection:** Protect seedlings outdoors from the worst of the weather and from insect pests and birds. Use horticultural fleece, cloches or netting supported on short stakes.

▶ **Potatoes:** Plant potatoes or start them off indoors for planting later on.

Late Spring

The Flower Garden

This is a favourite time in the garden for many gardeners, with flowers bursting out everywhere and the leaves of all plants still looking young and fresh.

Herb Gardens

Many people are attracted by the idea of growing herbs. Although you can incorporate culinary herbs in a kitchen garden, most herb gardens are designed to be decorative. If you don't have room for a dedicated herb garden, most can be successfully grown in containers.

A Herb Wheel

A wheel is a popular design, and looks very effective with a bird bath, stone ornament or large container (perhaps containing a bay or olive tree) at its centre. Plant up each segment of the wheel with a different herb, as follows:

▶ **Cane:** Decide on the centre spot and insert a cane at that point.

▶ **String:** Attach a string to the cane. Measure the desired radius on the string.

64

▶ **Bottle:** Tie an inverted plastic drinks bottle (or plastic cup with a small hole in the base) to the string.

▶ **Mark:** Fill the bottle or cup with sharp sand. Trace an arc, allowing the sand to trickle through to mark the circle.

▶ **Spokes:** Use straight canes to mark the spokes of the wheel.

Note: If you are making a large herb garden, the 'spokes' can be box hedges or even narrow paths.

Hedges

Give hedges their first cut of the year. If you are using powered equipment, be sure to follow all the relevant safety instructions.

▶ **A good cut:** To ensure an even cut, hold the blades of the shears or trimmer flat against the hedge.

▶ **Straight:** For an even line along the top of the hedge, stretch a length of string between two or more uprights at the appropriate height. Check the level with a spirit level.

▶ **Tidying up:** Reduce time spent clearing up the clippings by laying down a sheet next to the hedge you are about to cut.

▶ **Clippings:** Very soft deciduous clippings can go on the compost heap. If you are cutting the hedge back hard (into older, more woody growth), either shred the clippings (for composting) or burn them. Put the clippings from evergreen hedges in your green waste bin or burn them.

Note: Wood ash is one of the best organic sources of potash – a nutrient that many plants need to flower and fruit well. Spread the ash (when cool) around any fruit trees and bushes, and flowering shrubs such as roses and rhododendrons.

Wildlife Hedges

Prune any parts of the hedge that have just flowered and that you left untouched in early spring. Have a close look for any stems with developing fruits. You need to retain these to feed the birds later on. Cut back any new growth that might be shading them. Exposing the fruits to the sun will ensure that they ripen properly.

Sheep Shears

Sheep shears are an excellent tool for trimming box hedges and small topiary specimens. They can only be used effectively at this time of year, as they will only cut through very young, soft stems.

To attract wildlife, you need a good mix of deciduous plants and evergreens (to shelter birds and small mammals in winter). Plants with open, cup-shaped flowers draw in bees and other pollinating insects, while berries will feed birds in autumn and winter. Consider running *Clematis vitalba* (old man's beard) through the hedge – the fluffy seedheads provide birds with useful nesting material early in the year. Add an ivy, if you are short of evergreen material.

Plants For a Wildlife Hedge

Acer campestre (field maple) deciduous

Crataegus monogyna (hawthorn)
    deciduous, flowers, berries

Hedera helix (ivy)
    evergreen, flowers, berries

Ilex aquifolium (holly)
    evergreen, berries (on females)

Prunus spinosa (blackthorn, sloe)
    deciduous, flowers, fruits

Viburnum opulus (wayfarer tree)
    deciduous, flowers, berries

Prunus spinosa (blackthorn)

Note: Some gardeners include hazel (*Corylus*) in a wildlife hedge – but this has the disadvantage of attracting squirrels, a serious pest, into the garden.

Repairing a Hedge

Hedges sometimes show patches of die-back, which can be tackled now. Box (*Buxus*) and yew (*Taxus*) respond well to hard pruning, so don't be afraid to cut out all dead growth, down to the base, if necessary. Regrowth should be brisk, provided you feed and water well after cutting. Lavender (*Lavandula*) and rosemary (*Rosmarinus*) do not respond well to such severe treatment. Look for new shoots low down on the plant and cut back to these. If the plants are very woody and bare at the base, it is often better to replace them with new ones (see Making a Herb Hedge From Cuttings, p. 150).

Leylandii conifers often have brown patches near the base. Unfortunately, these plants cannot be pruned hard like yew. The best option is to cut out the dead material, then look for live stems at the same level on adjacent plants. Pull these across the dead area and tie them loosely in place. They will soon grow to conceal the gap.

Trees and Shrubs

Woody plants should be growing strongly now, particularly if the weather is damp and mild. For many, the spring show of flowers is already over and the plants are busy producing new stems for next year's show.

New Plantings

Check that all newly planted trees and shrubs are firmly anchored in the ground. The soil may have settled around them, making them unstable. Firm them in with your hands (or lightly with your heel), if necessary.

Japanese Maples

These dainty little trees (forms of *Acer japonicum* and *A. palmatum*) are a delight at this time of year, as the new leaves unfurl. They are very delicate, however, and can suffer during a night frost. Throw a fleece over them if a frost is predicted, removing this the following morning.

Pruning Shrubs

Prune shrubs that have finished flowering if you were unable to do this in early spring. Cut back older, very woody stems to the base, then shorten flowered stems by between one third and a half. Vigorous young stems can be left unpruned. After pruning, feed and water the plants well. Apply a mulch around the base in a doughnut-like ring to keep the roots cool over summer.

Note: Shrubs with a naturally neat habit, such as rhododendrons, need little pruning, if any.

Lilacs

Lilacs, grown for their gorgeously scented flowers, need to be dead-headed very carefully after the blooms have faded. With sharp secateurs, cut just below each flowerhead – next year's flower shoots are already starting to form just below them and they are easily damaged.

The First Rose of Summer

While – correctly – we think of roses as flowers of high summer, *R. xanthina* 'Canary Bird' is always in flower before the rest. The creamy yellow flowers offer a tantalizing foretaste of what is to come.

69

Roses

Flower buds are beginning to swell on all roses now. Continue to spray the plants against greenfly – either with an insecticide or a firm jet of water.

Climbers

Climbers are making vigorous growth now, especially if you gave them a hard prune earlier on in the year. Many are capable of producing 3 m (10 ft) of growth – or even more – in one growing season.

Training Climbers

Tie in the stems of all climbing plants as they grow. For optimum flowering, train main stems horizontally or in a fan arrangement. This encourages the plant to produce numerous side shoots, which will be flower-bearing.

Clematis

Take particular care when training clematis stems – they are very fragile and easy to break.

You can prune early-flowering *Clematis alpina* and *C. macropetala* now if they have become overgrown. Thin the stems to ease congestion, cutting older ones down to the base. Note that, if you prune very heavily, the plant may not flower the following year – though this is a very effective treatment for rejuvenating very old plants.

Clematis

Perennials

Many hardy perennials will be in flower now, including pulmonarias, peonies (*Paeonia*) and some of the hardy geraniums. Some provide good material for cutting for the house.

Top Tip

If you are using canes to stake perennials, cover the tip of each with a rubber cap to avoid eye injuries.

Ants on Peonies

Many gardeners are surprised to find ants crawling over the unopened buds of peonies. What attracts them is unknown – the ants seem to cause no damage either to the flowers or the plants.

Euphorbias

Take particular care if you need to cut back the stems on euphorbias that have flowered. They contain a milky latex that can cause irritation on contact with the skin. To avoid any risk, be sure to wear gloves when handling these plants.

Staking Perennials

Carry on staking perennials and dahlias. Tie tall stems to canes as they grow, using wire ties or short lengths of horticultural twine or raffia. Raise the discs on ring stakes to support the stems of peonies.

Paeonia (peony)

General Maintenance

Alongside all the maintenance on the plants, there are other jobs that need to be done in most gardens. The more time you devote to these now, the more time you'll have for relaxing in the summer.

Timber

A few days of warm, sunny, settled weather offer a good opportunity to assess the state of any timber in the garden – including fences, sheds, decking and seating. It is best to apply timber treatments in the morning, so that the product has a chance to dry before the evening (which may be damp). Choose a still day, so that the preservative does not blow on to nearby plants or into a garden pond. Apply wood preservative with a brush or (easier on fence panels and sheds) a pressure spray. Some preservatives are coloured, so you can use the same shade throughout the garden to create a sense of unity

Note: If you are applying colour to timber, it's only possible to darken it.

Paths and Paving

It's important to keep paths and paved areas clear of weeds and moss (which often appear in shade, or if the path does not drain easily). Not only is a clear path more attractive, but you are much less likely to lose your footing. Use a weedkiller formulated to keep paths clear. Many products are sold ready to use.

Top Tip

Use a spray algae cleaner to get rid of the slimy, greenish film you often see on paving slabs, decking, outdoor furniture, and stone and terracotta pots and garden features.

It can be difficult to eradicate deep-rooted weeds such as dandelions from between paving slabs. Treat these with a spot weedkiller painted directly on to the leaves or burn them off with a flame gun.

Garden Hoses

If you need to water the garden with a hose – to maintain a lawn or in the vegetable garden, for instance – check that all the fittings are fully watertight. Loose fittings are a common source of water loss. Tighten them fully or replace them if the threads are worn.

Composting

With the general rise in temperature, material in the compost heap starts to break down more rapidly. If your compost heap seems a bit cold, try adding a compost accelerator. These can either be sprinkled over each layer of fresh material you add or diluted for pouring over the heap.

Weed Control

Along with other garden plants, weeds will now be growing rampantly. Use a contact weedkiller to eliminate them. Treading on them or crushing them before applying the product can help absorption. A translocated weedkiller enters the plant's system and kills the plant from the inside – it does not enter the soil (any that lands on the soil breaks down naturally).

Note: Organic gardeners sometimes blanch at the idea of using weedkillers in the garden, but their use can be environmentally sound. If you pull up weeds by hand, you are also removing some of the topsoil, which contains plenty of microscopic life. Using a weedkiller means you do not have to disturb the soil.

Ponds

If you want to maintain a good ecological balance in the garden, a pond is particularly good at attracting wildlife. The water will attract frogs and toads, as well as a host of insect life, nearly all of it beneficial.

Stocking a Pond

This is a good time for adding new plants to a pond, as there is much less risk of the water freezing over than in the earlier part of the year. Bog plants and marginals can be planted in containers placed either on the shelves at the side of the pond or on bricks placed in the pond to achieve the appropriate depth.

▶ **Bog plants:** These plants need to have their roots in permanently moist water with their crowns above it.

▶ **Marginal plants:** These plants need about 7.5–15 cm (3–6 in) above their crowns.

▶ **Waterlilies:** Young waterlilies (*Nymphaea*) should be planted shallowly to begin with so that their juvenile leaves just float on the surface. Place the container on bricks to begin with. As the plant grows and the stems lengthen, you can gradually lower it until you achieve the final planting depth.

▶ **Oxygenating plants:** As with surface floaters, these plants do not need to be planted by any conventional method but can simply be introduced into the water.

Note: You can use ordinary garden soil for water plants grown in containers. It should not be manured, as the water in the pond contains plenty of microbial life that creates a suitable medium for the plant roots.

Water Snails

Water snails are unwelcome visitors to a pond, as they will eat the plants that are there. If the snails are near the edge of the pond, you may be able to reach in and collect them by hand. For a reliable method of trapping them, float a lettuce leaf on the surface of the water and leave this overnight. Lift the leaf the following morning and dispose of any snails that you find clinging to the underside.

75

Gardening Under Cover

This is a time for preparing seedlings and young plants before they go outside in early summer. With late frosts still possible in many areas, make full use of all the available space under cover.

Harden Off Seedlings

Start hardening off tender seedlings now. Place the containers outdoors in a spot sheltered from strong sun and wind, leaving them there for increasingly long periods. Bring them back under cover at night or put them in a cold frame (if a hard frost is forecast, cover the frame with a piece of old carpet or a thick blanket).

Plants From Seed and Tomatoes

It is not too late to sow seed for planting out later on in the year. Half-hardy annuals can be sown now to provide fills for gaps in beds and borders that you may notice in summer, or for containers and hanging baskets. You can also still sow tender crops such as tomatoes and cucumbers. Now is also the time to pot up young tomatoes, either that you have raised from seed yourself or bought as small plants.

Plant Hanging Baskets

You can get your hanging baskets off to a flying start now, so they are ready to hang outdoors once all danger of frost has passed. For the best display, cram the plants in.

Once planted, keep the basket in an unheated conservatory or porch.

▶ Basket: Set the unplanted basket in a bucket or large plant pot to stabilize it. Line the basket with moss (or a synthetic alternative).

▶ Plastic: Lay a sheet of thick black plastic (for instance, cut from an old potting compost bag) on top of the moss. Spike holes in the base of the plastic liner for good drainage.

▶ Compost: Put in a shallow layer of potting compost.

▶ Plant: Start to plant the sides of the basket. Make holes through the moss and plastic liner, then push the rootballs of the trailing plants in. Add a further layer of compost to cover the rootballs. Depending on the size of the basket, continue adding plants in at the sides.

▶ Top: Plant the top of the basket, using plants of a more rounded or upright habit.

▶ Feed: Add fertilizer pellets, water the basket well, and then allow to drain thoroughly before hanging up.

77

A Hanging Basket for a Shady Spot

Don't assume that a hanging basket has to be in full sun. It's perfectly possible to create an attractive planting for a shady wall. Suitable plants for a shady spot include:

▶ *Begonia*
▶ *Fuchsia*
▶ *Hedera*
▶ *Impatiens*
▶ *Lobelia*
▶ *Lysimachia*
▶ *Viola*

After watering the basket, leave it to drain thoroughly before hanging it outside – the weight of the water will make it difficult to lift.

Adding water-retaining gels to the compost reduces the risk of the planted basket drying out during the summer. Most hanging basket composts already contain the gel.

Trailing Plants for Hanging Baskets

Petunia

Begonia

Hedera

Helichrysum petiolare

Lobelia

Lotus berthelottii

Lysimachia

Pelargonium

Viola

Top Tip

While you can buy special hanging basket compost (which is intentionally very lightweight), it's easy to make your own. Simply mix multi-purpose compost with perlite or vermiculite – two-thirds compost by volume.

The Kitchen Garden

You will now be able to plant out seedlings you have raised in containers and begin harvesting early sowings. You can also carry on sowing quick-growing vegetables for use throughout the summer.

Runner Beans

Beans are a deservedly popular crop – easy to grow, the plants will produce pods over a number of weeks in summer and autumn. If you don't have much space, try growing dwarf bean varieties.

Supporting

Runner beans can be grown on a wigwam of canes about 2 m (6 ft) high. Alternatively, grow them in two parallel rows about 30 cm (12 in) apart. For growing in rows, drive pairs of canes into the soil, allowing about 30 cm (12 in) between pairs. Tie each pair together at the top about 15 cm (6 in) below the tips. Run a single cane along the top, tying this to each pair, as a support for the whole row.

Sowing

Sow one seed at the base of each cane. If late frosts are still likely, either delay planting for a few weeks or start the seeds off under cover for transplanting later.

Top Tip

A row of runner beans inevitably casts shade. Plant the shady side with leafy vegetables or salad crops that will appreciate the shelter from hot sun.

79

Intercropping

If you have rows of slow-maturing vegetables, such as Brussels sprouts and parsnips, you can now make use of the spaces in between for quick-growing salad crops – for instance, radishes and cut-and-come-again salad leaves. Sow them in drills between the other crops. Any thinnings can also be added to salads.

Beetroot

Beetroot is a versatile crop. While you can sow seed throughout the summer for small beets for immediate use, if you want large roots for storage over winter, sow now for harvesting in about 12 weeks' time. Sow the seed in drills, about 15–30 cm (6–12 in) apart – or more or less, depending on the variety chosen. Thin the seedlings as necessary.

Potatoes

Earth up potatoes as they grow. Mound up the soil around each stem when the plants are about 20 cm (8 in) tall. This prevents the tubers underground from turning green – and hence inedible.

Outdoor Tomatoes

Pre-germinated seeds can be sown outdoors in containers now, but protect them with a cloche or keep in a cold frame if you live in an area where late frosts are likely.

Start hardening off seedlings you have raised under cover by standing them outdoors for increasingly long periods during daylight hours. Bring them back under cover in the evening.

If you have bought small tomato plants from a garden centre, keep them under cover overnight until all risk of frost has passed.

Fruit

Many fruit trees and bushes are in flower now or just starting to develop their fruits. This is a critical period in their annual cycle.

Apples

Spraying apples and pears can protect them against a number of pests and diseases. Timing depends on to what degree the flowers are open – many flighted insect pests lay their eggs in the open flowers so that the developing fruit will be a food source for their larvae. Some gardeners prefer not to spray and look for varieties that are disease-resistant (though these will still be vulnerable to insect pests). If you do decide to treat your plants with a chemical, spray in the evening, when bees and other beneficial pollinating insects will not be active. Apple problems that can be controlled with sprays include:

- ▶ aphids
- ▶ apple sawfly
- ▶ codling moth
- ▶ fireblight
- ▶ mites
- ▶ powdery mildew
- ▶ rust
- ▶ scab

Peaches

Peaches are susceptible to peach leaf curl, a fungal disease. Leaves appear puckered and distorted. Pick off all affected leaves by hand and burn them (do not add them to the compost heap). Water the plant well to promote good recovery. The new crop of leaves should be unaffected.

Apple blossom

Peach blossom

82

Plants To Enjoy

Trees

Aesculus hippocastanum
  (horse chestnut)
Cercis siliquastrum
  (Judas tree)
Crataegus (hawthorn)
Cupressus macrocarpa
  'Goldcrest'
Laburnum
Malus (crab apple)
Pyrus calleryana 'Chanticleer'
  (ornamental pear)

Shrubs

Azara
Ceanothus (California lilac)
Choisya ternate
  (Mexican orange blossom)
Cistus (rock rose)
Coronilla
Cytisus (broom)
Daphne
Deutzia

Enkianthus
Euphorbia
Exochorda
Fothergilla
Kolkwitzia
Lavandula (lavender)
Leptospermum
  (New Zealand tea tree)
Mahonia
Osmanthus
Paeonia (tree peony)

Photinia
Pieris
Prunus lusitanica (Portugal laurel)
Rhododendron
Rosmarinus (rosemary)
Rubus 'Benenden'
Sophora
Syringa (lilac)
Viburnum
Weigela
Yucca

Cistus (rock rose)

83

Wisteria

Climbers

Actinidia kolomikta

Akebia quinata
  (chocolate vine)

Clematis montana

Clianthus (parrot's bill)

Humulus lupulus 'Aureus'
  (golden-leaved hop)

Lonicera (honeysuckle)

Wisteria

Perennials

Ajuga (bugle)

Astrantia

Aubrieta

Bergenia (elephant's ears)

Campanula

Centaurea

Convallaria
  (lily-of-the-valley)

Dicentra (bleeding heart)

Geranium

Geum

Hosta

Paeonia (peony)

Papaver (poppy)

Polygonatum
  (Solomon's seal)

Pulmonaria (lungwort)

Pulsatilla (Pasque flower)

Tiarella (foam flower)

Trollius (globe flower)

Veronica (speedwell)

Bulbs

Fritillaria (fritillary)

Tulipa (tulip)

Annuals and biennials

Myosotis (forget-me-not)

Trollius (globe flower)

84

Checklist

▶ **Shrubs:** Prune shrubs that have finished flowering. After pruning, feed them with a general fertilizer, water them, then apply a mulch of organic matter around the base.

▶ **Roses:** Watch out for greenfly on buds and young stems. Spray with an insecticide or dislodge them with a strong jet of water.

▶ **Climbers:** Train in new stems, as close to the horizontal as you can. Prune clematis if necessary.

▶ **Hedges:** Give established hedges their first cut of the season. Burn or shred the prunings.

▶ **Hanging baskets:** Plant up hanging baskets ready to put out when all danger of frost has passed.

▶ **Timber:** During still, dry weather, apply a wood preservative to fences, decking and the exterior of sheds.

▶ **Weeds:** Treat weeds with a weedkiller applied directly to the leaves.

▶ **Seeds:** Sow the seeds of half-hardy annuals. Start hardening off seedlings raised indoors by standing them outdoors for increasingly long periods during the daytime.

▶ **Potatoes:** Pile up the earth around the stems to exclude light from the potatoes just beneath the soil.

▶ **Apples and pears:** Spray apples and pears while they are in flower, to guard against certain pests and diseases. Apply the product in the evening, when pollinating bees are no longer active.

Early
Summer

The Flower Garden

As the longest day of the year approaches, the garden starts to take on a more mature, established look. While there are still jobs to be done, you can start to see the benefits of all the ones you tackled earlier in the year.

Convolvulus triclor (morning glory)

Trees and Shrubs

Most hardy trees and shrubs will have finished flowering by now, becoming backdrops to the perennials and annuals that are the main feature of the summer garden. But there is still some important maintenance work to be done.

Adding Interest to Shrub Borders

To add summer colour to a dull-looking shrubbery, plant a few annual climbers here and there, using the shrubs as supports. No formal training is required – just allow the climbers to find their own way through the branches. Suitable climbers include:

▶ Morning glory (*Convolvulus tricolor*)

▶ Chilean glory vine (*Eccremocarpus scaber*)

▶ Sweet peas (*Lathyrus odoratus*)

▶ Black-eyed Susan (*Thunbergia alata*)

Suckers

Most trees are grafted, so are not growing on their own roots but on the roots of a different but related tree (if you look near the base of the trunk, you'll see a tell-tale ring where the graft was made).

The rootstocks sometimes decide to start growing a new tree, either spontaneously or – more frequently – because the roots have been damaged in some way. This can happen if you have been digging around a tree, either to put in new plants or through routine soil improvement. The sucker can appear some distance away from the main trunk.

Cut off suckers from the base of the tree with sharp secateurs. If the sucker is away from the trunk, coming through the lawn or a flower bed, it's necessary to dig down to the point where the sucker meets the roots underground. Cut off the sucker from the root.

Thunbergia alata (black-eyed Susan)

Top Tip

As a change from their usual position by the front or back door, try suspending hanging baskets from sturdy and suitably placed branches on garden trees. Provided the leaf canopy is not too dense, they will provide a welcome splash of colour.

Water Shoots

Water shoots, which are similar to suckers, appear on the trunks of trees. Not only do they spoil the outline of the tree, but they can attract various insect pests. Rub them off with your finger and thumb as soon as you notice them. If they have developed as a stem, cut off at the trunk with sharp secateurs.

Pruning

This is the optimum time for pruning ornamental cherries and other members of the *Prunus* genus – a vast number of plants that includes plums, peaches and apricots. They are very susceptible to silver leaf, a fungal disease that enters plants through wounds (including pruning cuts) and is carried in rain water. During the long hours of sunlight at this time of year, pruning cuts heal rapidly, so the risk of infection is reduced.

After pruning, the plants need to be fed

Pruning of these plants is best kept to a minimum, however. Simply cut out dead, diseased and damaged material and shorten any overlong shoots that spoil the outline. Most ornamental cherries have a naturally pleasing shape that is easily spoilt.

Note: If the weather is wet during this season, you should delay pruning work on *Prunus* until a period of dry, sunny weather is forecast.

You can also prune late-spring-flowering shrubs such as weigelas and mock oranges (*Philadelphus*) now. Cut back flowered stems by up to one third or back to vigorous new shoots (which will flower next year, and will appreciate the space to grow). Very old and woody stems can be cut harder, down to ground level, if necessary. Thin the remaining stems, leaving very vigorous shoots unpruned.

After pruning, feed, water and mulch the plants well.

Shrubs with a naturally neat habit, such as Mexican orange blossom (*Choisya ternata*) and skimmias, need little pruning (if any).

Clematis – the Queen of Climbers

The main clematis season starts now – if you have the right conditions, you can have a clematis in flower virtually every day between now and early autumn. Clematis are usually divided into three groups, depending on when they flower. This is also a guide to how and when they should be pruned:

▶ **Group 1:** These plants flower during the first half of the year, mainly in early to mid-spring. The dainty *Clematis alpina* and *C. macropetala* belong to this group. The rampant *C. montana* is the last of the Group 1 clematis to flower.

▶ **Group 2:** This group consists of clematis that has two flushes of usually large flowers per year. The first crop opens in early summer, the second in late summer. Varieties with double flowers (e.g. 'Vyvyan Pennell') are particularly prized, but the second crop of flowers is usually single.

▶ **Group 3:** The largest group, this comprises large-flowered varieties such as 'Perle d'Azur', so-called *texensis* (e.g. 'Gravetye Beauty') and *viticella* (e.g. 'Polish Spirit') types, with smaller flowers, and some late-flowering species such as *C. tangutica* and *C. rehderiana*. Most flower from mid-summer to autumn.

91

Supporting Clematis

Nearly all clematis are climbing plants
that will need some form of support.
Good forms of support include:

▶ **Beds and borders:** Use a trellis
or metal obelisk or wigwam of
bamboo or canes.

▶ **Walls and fences:** Fix a trellis panel
or series of horizontal wires against
the wall or fence. If you are planting
a clematis – or any climber, for that
matter – against a wall or fence,
dig the planting hole about 30–45
cm (12–18 in) away from it. Angle
the top-growth towards the wall
or fence with the roots pointing
away. This is in order to minimize
the effect of the 'rain shadow' – the
area of soil at the foot of the wall
or fence that is sheltered from
heavy rain.

▶ **Posts:** Alternatively, stretch a length
of chicken or pig wire against two
fence posts, nailing it in position.

Planting Clematis

While you can plant clematis at any time when the soil is workable, you may well find yourself tempted by plants in flower sold at garden centres throughout the summer months.

▶ **Hole:** Dig a deep hole that will comfortably accommodate the rootball and the lower portion of the stems.

▶ **Cane:** Slide the clematis from its container and position it in the centre of the hole. Use a short cane or stick laid across the soil to gauge the correct planting depth. It's usual to bury a section of stem at the base of the clematis – about 10 cm (4 in). This encourages additional roots to develop along the portion of stem underground, resulting in a sturdier, more vigorous plant.

▶ **Roots:** If the roots are congested, gently tease them out with your fingers or with a hand fork.

▶ **Soil:** Backfill with the excavated soil. Shake the plant gently as you do so, to settle the soil around the roots.

▶ **Water:** Lightly firm the plant in with your hands, then water well.

93

Growing Tips for Clematis

Before planting a clematis, separate out the stems as far as possible – this will make them easier to tie in later.

Water the plant frequently during the first few weeks after planting, especially if the weather is dry.

Clematis prefer a neutral to alkaline soil.

They do well in positions where their roots are shaded – either by other, low-growing plants, by paving stones or by garden ornaments.

If you don't have the right soil, or are short on space, grow less vigorous varieties in large tubs or containers.

Train in stems as they grow, or they can soon become tangled.

Perennials

Perennials are the mainstay of the flower garden. The ones that have already flowered can become mere passengers at this time of year – sprucing them up will improve their health and appearance, and ensure they flower well next spring.

Dividing Primulas

Primulas that have finished flowering can be divided now. Dig up the clumps and cut them up into smaller pieces with a sharp knife. You can be ruthless about this – the plants respond well to this treatment. Replant the sections or pot them up for growing on.

Grooming Perennials

Many perennials have finished flowering now. Peonies should be dead-headed. Some other perennials will withstand harder treatment. Cut hardy geraniums, lupins (*Lupinus*) and poppies (*Papaver*) down to the ground. They will respond with a crop of fresh leaves, and some may even flower again later in the season. To improve the chances of a second flowering, feed the plants well with a liquid tomato fertilizer and keep well watered during dry weather.

Primulas

Acanthus leaves

Perennials with Good Foliage

Acanthus

Bergenia

Hosta

Paeonia (peonies)

Papaver (poppies)

Rheum

Thalictrum

95

Lilies

Keep watering lilies in pots as they grow – failure to maintain an adequate moisture supply will prevent the flower buds from developing properly. Keep an eye out for lily beetle. Beautiful red insects, they are a serious pest, rapidly eating their way through leaves and flower buds. Either spray with an insecticide or pick them off by hand and squash them.

Top Tip

Make a second sowing now of half-hardy annuals in containers, trays or modules. You can use these to replace ones you are planting out now in late summer. The later sowings will carry on flowering until the first frosts.

Bedding Plants

With all dangers of frosts over, it's safe to use plants that are not hardy in the garden. These include half-hardy bedding plants, either ones you have raised yourself from seed or bought as small plants from garden centres. Other plants in this category are a large group sometimes referred to as tender perennials. The beauty of tender perennials is that they have such a long flowering season. They will scarcely be without flowers between now and the first frosts.

Planting a Summer Container

If you are planting a large container, say 45 cm (18 in) deep or more, it's wasteful to fill the whole thing with potting compost, as the roots will only penetrate to a depth of 10–15 cm (4–6 in). Instead, half-fill the container with stones or chunks of polystyrene, then add compost. Alternatively, sink a shallow washing-up bowl (drill holes in the base for drainage) into the container.

▶ **Compost:** Put down a layer of compost. For improved drainage, replace up to one third of the compost with sharp sand or grit or the lighter-weight perlite and vermiculite.

▶ **Depth:** Check the depth by standing the plants on the compost surface still in their pots. Once planted, the compost level should be around 1–2 cm (½–1 in) of the container's rim, to allow for watering.

▶ **Plant:** When you are satisfied the level is correct, slide the plants from their containers and arrange them in the container. Most containers look best with a number of trailing plants around the edge (for suggestions, see 'Plant Hanging Baskets', p. 77).

▶ **Soil:** Sprinkle in compost between the rootballs to fill in the gaps.

▶ **Top-dress:** Water the container well. To improve the overall appearance and to keep the compost cool, sprinkle a layer of grit or sand over the surface.

Tender Perennials

Diascia
Felicia
Nemesia
Osteospermum
Pelargonium
Scaevola
Verbena

Hanging Baskets

Turn hanging baskets on their supports every week or so. This maintains even growth. Keep watering daily and feed with a fertilizer for flowering plants (or a tomato feed) – unless you added fertilizer pellets on planting.

Gardening Under Cover

Starting now, you need to keep a careful eye on all plants growing under cover, houseplants as well as ones in the greenhouse. On sunny days, the temperature can rise sharply, and certain pests and diseases can cause problems.

Tomatoes

Seedlings of outdoor tomatoes that you have kept under cover until now can go outside into their final positions – a sheltered, sunny spot. Pot up indoor varieties into large containers or growbags.

Growbags

You can also use growbags for plants other than tomatoes. For salad crops and herbs, cut a long panel in the top of the bag and sow the seeds in rows. Suitable plants include:

- aubergines
- basil
- chilli peppers
- courgettes
- cucumbers

- endive
- lettuce
- rocket
- sweet peppers

Watering and Feeding Tomatoes

Now the plants are growing strongly, keep them well watered and apply a tomato fertilizer once the fruits are set. Do not be tempted to overfeed, however, as this can spoil the flavour.

Cordon Tomatoes

Under glass, you can make the maximum amount of space by growing the plants as cordons. This produces tall plants that fruit abundantly without spreading too much sideways.

▶ **Support:** Tie the main stems as they grow to either bamboo canes inserted in the containers or to vertical strings stretched between the floor and the greenhouse roof.

▶ **More fruit:** Pinch out side shoots (which appear where the leaves meet the main stems) to divert the plant's energies into fruit production.

Note: Outdoor tomatoes can also be trained as cordons, but need to be in a spot sheltered from winds, as the plants tend to become top-heavy as the fruits are developing.

Taking Softwood Cuttings

You can increase your stock of many shrubs now, but they need to be rooted under cover. Always choose healthy, vigorous material from the parent plant.

▶ **Compost:** Prepare the rooting medium first. Fill pots with a mix of equal parts multi-purpose compost and sharp sand, water well and allow to drain.

▶ **Shoot:** Cut a non-flowering side shoot from the plant, cutting just above a leaf joint (or node).

▶ **Cutting:** Trim the base of the cutting just below a leaf joint and strip off the leaves from the lower half of the stem. Dip the cuttings in a fungicidal solution.

▶ **Plant:** Using a dibber or pencil to make planting holes, insert the cuttings in the compost. The lowest leaves on the cuttings should be just above the compost surface.

▶ **Propagate:** Label the cuttings with the name of the plant and the date, and then tent with a clear plastic bag.

To prevent the cuttings drying out too rapidly, put them in a plastic bag before dealing with them.

Softwood cuttings are susceptible to rotting. Make sure all surfaces and tools are clean by wiping them with a plant-friendly disinfectant before use. If you have no suitable disinfectant or fungicide within easy reach, just add a splash of mouthwash to a bowl of water and use that instead.

You can improvise a mini-propagator by cutting a clear plastic drink bottle in half. Either half (the base inverted) will fit over a small container. The upper half has the advantage in that you can take the lid on and off to control the temperature and humidity.

Aftercare

Keep the cuttings in a light position, but out of direct sunlight. They

> ## Top Tip
> Take softwood cuttings
> early in the morning while
> the stems are still firm from
> overnight dew.

will root faster if you keep the compost warm. Either stand the pots on the tray of a heated propagator or place them near (but not on top of) a radiator.

While the cover will fog up readily – important to keep the cuttings firm – you need to keep a careful watch that there is not too much water condensing on the leaves. Remove the covers regularly and wipe them out or replace them with fresh ones.

Greenhouses

If you have a greenhouse, keep a close eye on the temperature, which can rise steeply during sunny weather. The glass magnifies the sunlight. As far as possible, rotate all the plants, so that they have equal access to the light – otherwise they can become leggy. Make sure that leaves are not touching the glass.

Staying Cool

On warm, sunny days, open all the vents and the greenhouse door. While this effectively lowers the temperature, it also allows pests into the greenhouse. Watch out for wasps and slugs. Frogs may also wander in, as may less welcome mice. Set traps for the latter, if necessary.

During a period of hot weather, hose down the greenhouse floor in the evenings. This lowers the temperature, as well as creating humidity around the plants.

101

The Kitchen Garden

You will really start to appreciate your earlier efforts now, as you begin to bring in crops almost on a daily basis. You can also carry on sowing quick-developing crops.

Potatoes

Carry on earthing up potatoes as the stems grow. With a hoe or your hands, draw the surrounding soil up around the stems.

Seedling Vegetables

Thin the seedlings of any crop you sowed in late spring (some of these thinnings make useful additions to salads).

Vegetables in Containers

If you don't have room for a dedicated vegetable plot, or would just like to have a few vegetables on the patio for immediate use, there are many that are suitable for growing in containers. Most should be sown in modules initially, but cut-and-come-again salad crops can be sown direct in the container. Use large containers, at least 45 cm (18 in)

across and deep. Soil-based composts (John Innes No.2 or No.3), or special organic vegetable composts, yield the best crops. Water the containers regularly – the compost should not be allowed to dry out. Dwarf varieties of the following are ideal for container-growing:

- ▶ aubergines
- ▶ beetroot
- ▶ lettuces
- ▶ peppers
- ▶ radishes
- ▶ spinach beet
- ▶ tomatoes

If you want to grow runner beans in a container, choose less vigorous varieties.

Top Tip

To get good results from all your leafy vegetables, feed them with an organic, seaweed-based fertilizer.

Edible Hanging Baskets

If you are really short of space, there are a number of crops suitable for use in hanging baskets. Some tomato varieties (e.g. 'Tumbling Ted') have been specially bred for this purpose, with clusters of small fruits on trailing stems. You can also try compact strawberry plants.

Hang the baskets in a sunny, sheltered position. Water the plants well, and feed with a tomato fertilizer (also beneficial for strawberries). The compost should not be allowed to dry out.

Herbs

Start picking leaves from herbs for use fresh in cooking and in salads. Use scissors to cut woody stems. The plants will keep on producing throughout the summer. Many herbs are aromatic plants of the Mediterranean that have adapted to grow in poor soils. Unlike other crops, most herbs do not need additional feeding.

Basil

Basil is one of the most popular of all herbs, and the flavour of home-grown plants is vastly superior to shop-bought ones. It is half-hardy, so seed should be sown indoors initially, though seedlings can be grown on outdoors now that there is no danger of late frosts.

Basil is best grown in containers filled with gritty compost. Water the plants well and feed with a seaweed-based fertilizer. They need a sunny, sheltered spot – some gardeners like to place the pots next to their tomato plants, so they can pick the leaves along with the ripe fruits for an instant salad.

Strawberries

Protect ripening fruits from mud splashes by placing straw or special strawberry mats around the plants to lift them off the soil. To protect them from birds, spread a net over them, supported on short stakes positioned at each corner of the strawberry bed. You may also need to set traps against mice.

Plants To Enjoy

Trees

Cornus kousa

Laburnum

Paulownia (foxglove tree)

Populus x Canadensis (poplar)

Shrubs

Aloysia

Azara

Berberis darwinii

Buddleja alternifolia

Callistemon

Carpenteria

Ceanothus (California lilac)

Choisya ternate
  (Mexican orange blossom)

Cistus (rock rose)

Colutea

Coronilla

Cytisus battandieri (Moroccan
  broom, pineapple broom)

Daphne

Deutzia

Euphorbia

Exochorda

Fremontodendron

Genista (broom)

Hebe

Kalmia (calico bush)

Kolkwitzia

Lavandula (lavender)

Leptospermum
  (New Zealand
  tea tree)

Ligustrum (privet)

Ozothamnus

Paeonia (tree peony)

Philadelphus
  (mock orange)

Potentilla

Prunus lusitanica
  (Portugal laurel)

Rhododendron

Rosa (rose)

Rosmarinus (rosemary)

Rubus 'Benenden'

Sophora

Spiraea

Viburnum

Weigela

Yucca

Climbers

Actinidia kolomikta

Clianthus (parrot's bill)

Humulus lupulus 'Aureus'
  (golden-leaved hop)

Hydrangea petiolaris
  (climbing hydrangea)

Lathyrus grandiflorus
  (everlasting pea)

Lonicera (honeysuckle)

Passiflora
  (passion flower)

Rosa (rose)

Perennials

Achillea

Alchemilla mollis (lady's mantle)

105

Hemerocallis (daylily)

Astrantia

Campanula (bell flower)

Dianthus (carnation, pink)

Dicentra (bleeding heart)

Geranium

Geum

Hemerocallis (daylily)

Hosta

Iris

Lupinus (lupin)

Paeonia (peony)

Papaver (poppy)

Primula

Rodgersia

Verbascum

Bulbs

Allium (ornamental onion)

Fritillaria (fritillary)

Nectaroscordum

Annuals and Biennials

Aquilegia (granny's bonnets)

Begonia

Godetia

Matthiola (stock)

Petunia

Tagetes (African marigold, French marigold)

Matthiola incana (stock)

106

Checklist

▶ **Suckers:** Remove suckers from around the base of trees and shrubs. Dig down to the roots, if necessary, so that the suckers do not grow back again.

▶ **Pruning:** Prune shrubs that flowered in late spring. This is also the best time to prune peaches, plums, cherries and other ornamental members of the *Prunus* genus.

▶ **Take cuttings:** Take softwood cuttings of a range of shrubs. Keep them well protected and maintain humid conditions while they are rooting.

▶ **Perennials:** Remove the faded flower stems of perennials that have already flowered. Cut back poppies and hardy geraniums to encourage a fresh crop of flowers.

▶ **Bedding plants:** Plant out bedding plants, either bought from a garden centre or raised at home, to fill gaps in beds and borders, and in containers and hanging baskets for summer.

▶ **Tomatoes:** Plant outdoor tomatoes outside, either in large containers or growbags. Support plants on canes or – if you are growing them in a greenhouse – on vertical strings.

▶ **Vegetables:** Thin the emerging seedlings of crops you have sown in drills.

▶ **Herbs:** Start harvesting the leaves of herbs to keep them producing and to prevent them flowering.

▶ **Strawberries:** Protect the fruits from mud splashes with special mats or by spreading straw underneath them. Net them to keep off birds.

Mid-Summer

The Flower Garden

This is the peak season of the gardening year. The garden is full of colour now, with roses, perennials and many annuals flowering for weeks on end.

Lawns

Mow lawns regularly. During a dry spell, water the lawn with a sprinkler in the evenings. If a garden-hose ban is in force, either use rainwater collected in a water butt (if you can spare it) or – probably the better solution – leave the grass unmown. Although it may well turn brown during hot weather, it will soon recover the next time it rains.

Birds

While the garden may be full of birds, water may be in short supply. If you have a bird bath, keep it topped up – most are very shallow and dry out rapidly.

Conserving Water

Water is a precious resource, particularly at this time of year, as the soil dries out during the long periods of dry, sunny days. Install water butts wherever you can – to catch water from greenhouse, shed and garage roofs, as well as from the house. All guttering and downpipes should be plastic. Iron guttering will contaminate the water.

Grey Water

So-called because of its cloudy appearance, grey water is waste water from domestic activities such as laundry, dishwashing, and baths, showers and basins. It can be collected via a separated plumbing system for use in the garden. Since grey water has usually been heated, it should be allowed to cool before use. But it should be used as soon as possible after collection, as the micro-organisms in it will start to putrefy it.

If you prefer not to use recycled water in the kitchen garden (because of chemicals in soaps and detergents), use it on ornamental plants or to refresh the lawn.

Note: Grey water is never safe to drink.

Trees and Shrubs

During warm weather, growth slows down. On warm, sunny days, new stems start to thicken and harden. This is an important time in the lifecycle of winter-flowering shrubs, as they are already starting to build next year's flowers.

Roses

All roses benefit from heavy watering during this period, especially varieties that will have a second flowering in late summer to autumn. Other maintenance tasks for roses include:

▶ **Flowers:** Remove the faded flowers from all roses, unless you are growing them for their decorative autumn hips. After dead-heading, fork in a rose fertilizer around the base of each plant, water well and mulch.

▶ **Stems:** Tie in the stems of climbing roses as they grow. Train the stems as close to the horizontal as you can. If the stems are very stiff, pull them into a rough fan shape.

▶ **Train:** To cover the uprights of a pergola or arch (or to train on a tripod or obelisk), train the stems round in a spiral.

Note: Training the main stems of roses and other climbing plants horizontally encourages the plant to push out short side shoots all along the length of the stem. These shorter shoots will be flower-bearing.

Taking Cuttings

Carry on taking softwood cuttings of shrubs (see p. 99), particularly of those that have only recently finished flowering, such as mock oranges (*Philadelphus*). As the stems are still soft and flexible, and susceptible to moisture loss, root them in a protected environment under cover.

Layering

As an alternative to taking cuttings, you can try layering shrubs instead. As a propagation method, this is virtually fool-proof, and minimal aftercare is involved. However, it's usually possible to create only a couple of new plants using this technique and the layers can be slow to produce roots.

▶ **Branch:** Bring a vigorous but flexible, low-growing branch down to soil level. Locate a point on the stem about 15–30 cm (6–12 in) from the tip, between leaves, which will touch the ground.

▶ **Hole:** Dig a shallow hole in the soil where the stem touches the ground.

▶ **Stem:** Bend the stem down so it touches the soil. You may need to remove some of the leaves to either side of the bend. Hold the stem in position with a short length of stout wire bent into a U-shape.

▶ **Soil:** Cover the stem with the excavated soil.

▶ **Cane:** If possible, bend the end of the stem upright and attach it to a short cane driven into the soil next to it. This not only marks the layer, but also encourages the stem to grow upright.

▶ **Pot up:** Layers should root in around 6–12 months. Once rooted, cut the stem back beyond the rooted section and dig it up. Pot it up in potting compost or move it to another part of the garden.

Shrubs Suitable for Layering

Aucuba (spotted laurel)
Chaenomeles (japonica, ornamental quince)
Daphne blagayana
Erica (heath)
Kalmia (calico bush)
Laurus (bay)
Magnolia
Osmanthus
Rhododendron
Skimmia
Syringa (lilac)

Chaenomeles (japonica, ornamental quince)

113

Climbers

Climbers are vigorous plants. Keep them well watered to
maintain even growth. Tie in the stems of climbers such
as wisteria as they grow (particularly important on young
plants, to extend the framework).

Clematis Care

Remove the faded flowers from the first flush on Group
2 varieties (see p. 91) – buds of the second flush should
already be developing. Thin the stems of all clematis,
especially if they are congested – a major cause of mildew
and other fungal diseases later on. Water the plants well
and apply a thick mulch around the base of the plant both
to conserve moisture in the soil and to keep the roots cool.

Wisteria

Perennials

Several hardy perennials have finished flowering now, and
will not flower again until next year. A bit of attention now
will freshen them up ready for next year.

Hellebores

If you grow hellebores, and would like to have more,
collect the seed now. Seed is ready when the seed cases
at the centre of each flower start to dry out, turn brown and

Hellebore, showing seed

114

Helleborus caucasicus (oriental hellebore)

split. Sow the seed straight away – it does not store well and germinates best when fresh. Fill small pots with seed compost (or multi-purpose compost), lay the seeds on top, and then top with a layer of grit. Hellebores are hardy plants, so the pots can simply be placed outdoors, but in a sheltered position.

If you do not wish to grow hellebores from seed, cut off all faded flowers. This will divert the plant's energies away from seed production and into growth, giving you a bigger plant.

Note: Hellebores are usually grown from seed, as, unlike most other perennials, the clumps are not easy to divide into sections.

Dividing Irises

Border irises that have finished flowering can be divided now. These are the so-called rhizomatous irises (a rhizome being a swollen root with a tendency to grow horizontally). If your clump is congested, with lots of leaves and not many flowers, dividing it will improve flowering next year.

▶ Rhizome: Dig up the rhizomes with a garden fork. Take care not to drive in the fork too close to the rhizome or you may damage it. Cut back any flowered stems.

▶ Clean: Shake or wash the roots free of loose soil. Depending on its size and age, the clump may fall apart into smaller, more manageable pieces in your hands.

▶ Cut: Cut off any older, rotted or damaged parts of the rhizome, then cut the remaining rhizome into pieces, each with a sheaf of healthy leaves.

115

▶ **Roots:** Trim back any long roots. Reduce the length of the leaves to about 15 cm (6 in), cutting them in a mitre shape. (The divisions will be top-heavy otherwise, and a strong wind can dislodge them from their planting position.)

▶ **Fungicide:** To guard against possible infection, dust the cut surfaces of the rhizome with a powdered fungicide.

▶ **Plant:** Replant the divisions – the upper surface of the rhizome should be just above the soil surface.

Bulbs

While autumn and spring are the traditional bulb-planting seasons, there are a few valuable autumn-flowering bulbs that can be planted now. Like the spring bulbs, they are most effective when planted in bold clumps.

Autumn Crocuses

Confusingly, autumn crocuses are not crocuses but an unrelated plant, *Colchicum autumnale.* Their goblet-like flowers (pink or white) look good in drifts in lawns. To naturalize bulbs in grass:

▶ **Plan:** Scatter the bulbs across the grass to ensure an informal look.

▶ **Hole:** Remove a plug of soil where each bulb has landed, either with a trowel or a special bulb planter.

▶ **Plant:** Remove a little soil from the base of the hole to accommodate the bulb. Put one bulb at the base of each hole, and then replace the plug. Firm in to restore the level of the lawn.

Note: Colchicums produce their flowers before the leaves. These appear the following spring and should be allowed to develop and die back. If you need to mow the lawn while they are above ground, mow round them.

Hanging Baskets

Continue carrying out important maintenance tasks and your hanging baskets will reward you with flowers:

▶ **Turn:** Keep turning baskets regularly to ensure even growth.

▶ **Water and feed:** Water daily and feed regularly with a tomato fertilizer or flowering plant fertilizer.

▶ **Dead-head:** Remove flowers as they fade. This not only keeps disease at bay, but also encourages the plants to produce more flowers.

117

Ponds

During hot, dry weather, ponds lose water rapidly. It's important to keep them topped up, not only for the obvious reason of maintaining the water level, but because the pH of the water can fluctuate wildly if you allow it to drop significantly and then introduce fresh water from the mains.

If you are filling a pond with a hose, hold the end above the water level so that the water splashes. This agitates the water and helps oxygenate it.

If you have a fountain in the pool, turn it on in the evening following a hot day – this will also oxygenate the water.

Algae

Algae – a green slime – builds up during hot weather in summer. It can often proliferate in a new pond, where there are not enough submerged oxygenating plants (see opposite) and waterlilies are not mature – ideally, their floating leaves should cover up to three quarters of the water surface in summer, thus keeping the water cool. Most garden ponds are self-regulating and intervention can cause more harm than good. Check the water for dead and decaying leaves, and remove these. To clear the water of algae quickly, use an ultraviolet (uV) clarifier.

Algae in a pond

Pond Weeds

Pond weeds make excellent additions to the compost heap. Look out for the following weeds in your pond:

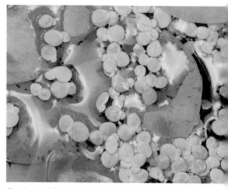

Duckweed (Lemna)

▶ Blanket weed (*Spirogyra*): This plant grows beneath the water surface in dense strands, with growth being particularly vigorous in summer. You may not realize it is causing a problem until it comes to the surface, where it accumulates in unsightly masses. Remove it by holding a cane or length of bamboo in the water, then twisting this so that the weed wraps around it like candy floss.

▶ Duckweed (*Lemna*): This is a tiny, two-leaved plant that floats on the water surface with its roots trailing below. Usually brought in on the feet of birds, it will rapidly colonize a small pond. Remove it with a shrimp net.

Oxygenating Plants

These plants grow beneath the water surface. They absorb excess mineral salts in the water and starve out algae, as well as giving out oxygen and providing a shelter for pond life. However, they can get out of hand in summer and may need controlling. Pull out clumps with your hands, making sure you leave enough behind to maintain water clarity. It's best to thin little and often throughout the warm months, while the plants are growing strongly. Oxygenating plants include:

▶ *Callitriche verna*

▶ *Elodea crispa*

▶ *Fontinalis antipyretica* (water moss, willow moss)

▶ *Hottonia palustris* (water violet)

▶ *Potanogeton crispus* (curled pondweed)

▶ *Ranunculus aquatilis* (water crowfoot)

119

Gardening Under Cover

Although you will want to spend most of your time outdoors at this time of year, all plants under cover need close attention. This applies particularly to greenhouse crops.

Orchids

If you grow cymbidium orchids, place them outdoors now for the summer. Choose a shaded, sheltered spot. This helps firm the growth and avoids a build-up of pests such as scale insects. If you grow *Phalaenopsis* (moth orchids), keep removing the faded flowers. Once a whole truss has faded, shorten the stem, cutting just above a node (noticeable as a little kink on the stem). New flowering shoots will develop from these.

Water orchids frequently during this period, but make sure that all excess water can drain freely from the containers.

In the Greenhouse

During these long summer days, greenhouse plants thrive – but so do many pests (see p. 123). You need to maintain a clean, stable environment for good results from any crops that you are growing.

Preventing Problems

Make sure plants are not overcrowded in the greenhouse. Adjacent plants
should not touch each other – which allows insect pests and disease to
spread – and should also not touch the glass. Turn plants to maintain even
growth. Promptly remove any dry, scorched or shed leaves, both from the
plants themselves and from the staging and floor. These can shelter pests and
be a growing medium for fungal diseases.

Staying Cool

To prevent temperatures rising too high too quickly in a greenhouse, which puts plants
under undue stress, you need to shade the glass. You can either apply a wash directly to
the glass (which can be removed later in the year) or stretch a mesh over the inside of the
roof to filter the light. Continue to maintain good ventilation by opening all windows and the door during hot,
dry weather. Hose down the floor during the evenings (also in the mornings during particularly warm spells).

Tomatoes

Indoor tomatoes will come into flower now. Keep a watch out for early signs of pests and diseases
(see p. 123) on plants and deal with these promptly.

▶ **Cordons:** On cordons, remove side shoots that emerge from the leaf joints on the main stem. Pinch
   them out with finger and thumb (or use sharp scissors) when they are about 2.5 cm (1 in) long.

▶ **Shake or spray:** To ensure pollination (vital if fruits are to follow the flowers), you need to disperse
   the pollen. While they are in flower, either shake the plants daily or spray them with water.

▶ **Water:** Keep the plants well watered without waterlogging them – all excess water should drain
   away freely.

121

Aubergines

Maintain good humidity around the plants
through regular misting. Once the plants are
about 30 cm (12 in) tall, pinch out the growing
tips with finger and thumb, according to the
following simple rules:

▶ Allow only one fruit to develop on each shoot.

▶ Count three leaves beyond each selected
fruit, and then pinch out the stem tip.

Melons

To train melon plants, tie the stems to horizontal
strings or wires. To ensure good fruiting, transfer
the pollen from the male flowers to the female
flowers with a small paintbrush. Pinch back
the side shoots to two leaves beyond each
developing fruit.

Cucumbers

Cucumbers can develop their fruits without
being pollinated – and pollination is undesirable,
in fact, as it results in bitter-tasting fruits. To
prevent pollination, pinch out male flowers on
cucumber plants (unless you are growing
all-female varieties).

Greenhouse Pests and Diseases

Insect pests are particularly troublesome during the summer months, as most are capable of breeding quickly to produce plagues. Fungal diseases can also be a problem. Keep a watch out for symptoms and deal with any pest or disease as soon as you spot any damage. The following are likely to occur:

Botrytis cinerea, or grey mould

▶ **Red spider mite:** These mites are a serious pest under glass. They spin fine silk webs between leaves and stems. During warm weather, they can migrate to plants outdoors. Chemical controls are rarely successful. Mist the plants regularly to increase humidity (which suppresses reproduction). The predatory mite *Phytoseiulus persimilis* (available by mail order) can be effective.

▶ **White fly:** Tiny, moth-like creatures that lay their eggs on the undersides of leaves. Yellow mottling appears on the leaf surfaces. Control them with an insecticide or the parasitic wasp *Encarsia formosa*.

▶ **Thrips:** Adults are winged and black, while the young nymphs are wingless and creamy yellow. They cause a silvery discoloration to appear on leaves and can spread viruses. Control them with an insecticide or catch them using sticky traps.

▶ **Botrytis:** Also known as grey mould, this is common under glass and is rapidly spread from plant to plant. It proliferates in wet conditions. A grey-brown fluff appears on fruits, stems and leaves. Cut back affected growth and make sure there is sufficient space between plants to maintain good air circulation.

123

The Kitchen Garden

In most gardens, this is the start of the fruit season. There are also early potatoes and leafy vegetables and salads to enjoy. You will be beginning to harvest delicious crops daily.

General Maintenance

For good crops, it's vital to maintain an even water supply. Any check in growth can spoil the flavour and may even result in the loss of the crop. Water vegetables and fruit bushes regularly. Remove all annual weeds promptly – not only do these compete with the cropping plants for available water, but they attract pests into the garden and are often hosts to fungal diseases. All diseased weeds should be burnt. Others can be added to the compost heap.

Vegetables

Few gardeners begrudge the time spent in the vegetable plot at this time of year. The growing results around you remind you of the rewards for all your labours.

Potatoes

Harvest early potatoes as the plants begin to flower (or just before). Maincrop varieties can stay in the ground until the autumn.

Beans

Harvest early sowings of runner beans and French beans. The plants will carry on producing throughout the summer.

Brussels Sprouts

Brussels sprouts are taller plants than most vegetables. For extra stability (particularly in a windy garden), either draw up the soil around the lower parts of the stems or stake individual plants with short canes.

Salad Crops

You can continue to sow cut-and-come-again lettuces and rocket to provide leaves from late summer into autumn. Sow directly in drills or raise in containers. Carry on harvesting the crops from seed sown earlier in the year.

Outdoor Tomatoes

Water tomatoes in containers regularly. During dry spells, it may be necessary to water twice a day, both in the evening and early morning. To make the maximum use of water, apply the water from a can (without a rose) directly into the containers – water from a spray will evaporate more quickly, so less is available to the plants. Feed well with a tomato fertilizer applied at the recommended rate.

125

Courgettes

Keep picking courgettes while they are still small. Any left on the plant will develop as marrows. Keep the plants well watered to ensure that the fruits swell evenly.

Fruit

There's nothing nicer than picking fruit straight from the bush with the warmth of the sun still on it. Most soft fruits are ripening, and between now and autumn scarcely a week will go by without some fresh fruit for eating either straight from the tree or for cooking or jam-making.

Apples

It's usual for apple trees to shed some of their fruits at this time of year. This is normal and does not indicate anything is wrong – the tree is naturally shedding fruits that it does not have the energy to carry. Gather all fallen fruits from around the base of the tree. They are generally too small for eating or cooking, but can be added to the compost heap.

Plums

Plum trees often fruit prolifically, usually to the detriment of the crop and the overall well-being of the tree itself. If fruits are crowded on the stems, they do not have sufficient space to swell fully – also, where the fruits rub against each other, rots can occur and the skin can split. Heavy crops weigh branches down. Not only can this result in fruits trailing on the ground, but the branches themselves can rip from the trunk. To safeguard against possible problems, try to do the following:

▶ Thin clusters of fruits using scissors.

▶ Support heavily laden branches by driving
stout stakes into the ground and lashing branches
to them.

Soft Fruits

Harvest the fruits of white, red and black currants. Cut off entire fruit trusses
with scissors or secateurs, and then strip off the currants into a bowl using a
kitchen fork or your fingers. Gooseberries are also ripening now. They can usually
be picked by hand. (Wear gloves, if you have not selected a thornless variety.)

Summer Raspberries

Harvest the berries by hand. Once all the crop has been
picked, cut the stems (or canes) that have carried the fruit
down to ground level.
There should already
be new shoots from
the base of the plant
that will fruit next year.
Leave these unpruned,
but, if they are crowded,
thin them, cutting out
the less vigorous stems.
After pruning, feed
the plants, water well
and mulch.

127

Blueberries

Protect the developing fruits from birds by netting the bushes. If you are growing the plants in containers, keep them well watered.

Figs

Fig trees are fully hardy, but crop reliably only in areas with hot summers. To grow them successfully in cool areas, they need a sheltered position that receives a lot of sunlight – near or against a warm wall is ideal if the fruits are to ripen fully. Figs should be grown in large containers. They are vigorous plants, and restricting the root growth in this way stunts the growth and encourages fruit production. (Grown in the open ground, a fig will make a large tree that will not fruit well.) Use a soil-based compost (John Innes No.3). Water the container regularly during spring and summer when the plant is growing strongly.

Young fig plant

Prune figs now, with care – the stems bleed a milky sap that can cause an allergic reaction. Wear gloves and start at the base of the plant, working your way upwards, so that the sap does not drip on to leaves below. Shorten all new stems. The aim is not only to restrict growth, but to expose the fruits – which should be clearly visible – to the sun.

Did You Know?

Figs do not flower and fruit in the usual way. The figs you eat are not technically fruits but flower clusters turned inside out.

Plants To Enjoy

Trees

Catalpa bignoniodes
   (Indian bean tree)
Liriodendron tulipifera
   (tulip tree)
Magnolia grandiflora
   (bull bay)

Buddleja davidii (butterfly bush)

Shrubs

Abelia
Buddleja davidii
   (butterfly bush)
Carpenteria
Ceanothus (California lilac)
Cestrum parqui
Cistus (rock rose)
Colutea
Cytisus battandieri (Moroccan
   broom, pineapple broom)
Elaeagnus 'Quicksilver'
Escallonia
Fuchsia
Hebe
Hydrangea
Hypericum (rose of Sharon)
Hyssopus (hyssop)
Lavandula (lavender)
Myrtus (myrtle)
Olearia (daisy bush)
Philadelphus (mock orange)
Phlomis

Rosa (rose)

Phygelius
Potentilla
Rosa (rose)
Rosmarinus (rosemary)
Spiraea
Yucca

129

Dahlia

Climbers

Actinidia kolomikta

Clematis

Eccremocarpus scaber
  (Chilean glory flower)

Ipomoea (morning glory)

Humulus lupulus 'Aureus'
  (golden-leaved hop)

Lathyrus grandiflorus
  (everlasting pea)

Lonicera (honeysuckle)

Polygonum (Russian vine)

Rosa (rose)

Solanum jasminoides 'Album'

Trachelospermum jasminoides
  (star jasmine)

Perennials

Acanthus (bear's breeches)

Achillea

Astrantia

Delphinium

Felicia

Geranium

Hemerocallis (daylily)

Hosta

Kniphofia (red hot poker)

Nemesia

Osteospermum

Pelargonium

Bulbs

Crocosmia

Dahlia

Lilium (lily)

Annuals and biennials

Alyssum

Antirrhinum (snapdragon)

Calendula (pot marigold)

Lathyrus odoratus
  (sweet pea)

Lobelia

Matthiola (stock)

Mesembryanthemum
  (Livingstone daisy)

Nicotiana (tobacco plant)

Petunia

Tagetes (African marigold,
  French marigold)

130

Checklist

▶ **Lawns:** During periods of drought, water lawns to keep them green. Alternatively, leave them unmown until after it has rained again.

▶ **Roses:** Remove the faded flowers from repeat-flowering roses to be sure of a good display later in the season. Leave them on varieties that have decorative autumn hips.

▶ **Irises:** Divide border irises with thick rhizomes.

▶ **Bulbs:** Plant autumn crocuses (*Colchicum*), either in drifts in the lawn or to fill bare patches around established shrubs.

▶ **Ponds:** During hot weather, maintain the water level in ponds. Splash the water in during the evening in order to oxygenate the water. Deal with pond weeds and thin oxygenating plants as necessary.

▶ **Greenhouses:** Apply a wash to the roof (or use shading fabric) to reduce the heat under the glass. Ventilate the house on hot days. Hose down the floor in the evening. Turn plants and do not crowd.

▶ **Vegetables:** Keep vegetable plants well watered during hot, dry weather so they grow at an even rate.

▶ **Potatoes:** Harvest early potatoes.

▶ **Salads:** Harvest the leaves of cut-and-come-again leafy vegetables. Carry on sowing seeds for replacements later in the season.

131

Late
Summer

The Flower Garden

This period – sometimes called the 'dog days' of summer – is often the hottest time of the year. And it's also the time when many people take their holidays, particularly if they have children.

Hedges

Hedges should have their second cut of the year now. Use shears or a powered hedge trimmer, as the growth will be very firm if the summer has been hot and dry. The clippings can be either shredded (then added to the compost heap) or burnt – the cold ash makes an excellent organic fertilizer for fruit bushes. Gardeners often neglect to feed their hedges, but they have the same needs as other plants in the garden. After cutting the hedge, fork in a general fertilizer around the base of each plant, water well and then mulch.

Did You Know?

The majority of domestic accidents occur in the garden. If you are using a stepladder to clip a hedge, be sure that it is firmly anchored on the ground. Take particular care when using any powered machinery and wear appropriate safety clothing at all times.

Anthemis tinctoria (golden marguerite)

Wildlife

On warm, sunny days, the garden will be alive with pollinating insects, especially if you grow lots of annuals and other late-summer-flowering plants. Hoverflies (which feed on aphids and mealy bugs) are particularly attracted to yellow flowers. Plants with yellow flowers include:

- ▶ *Achillea* (yarrow)
- ▶ *Alyssum saxatilis*
- ▶ *Anthemis tinctoria* (golden marguerite)
- ▶ *Hypericum*
- ▶ *Limnanthes douglasii* (poached egg plant)
- ▶ *Solidago* (golden rod)
- ▶ *Zinnia*

Frogs and toads

While you may appreciate the warm weather, frogs and toads generally do not. If you can leave an area of the garden – however small – uncultivated, these amphibians will relish the shelter of tall grass and weeds. Otherwise, a pile of large stones, with shady nooks and crannies, may be equally appreciated.

135

Pyracanthas

If you have a pyracantha growing against a wall, formally trained or not, cut back some of the new leafy growth that may be shading the berries. This will expose them to the light, ensuring that they ripen fully.

Climbers

Keep tying in the new growth of all climbers, especially wisteria, to extend the framework.

Roses

Some roses will be having a rest now, either having finished flowering altogether or building up their reserves for a second flush of flowers. Keep an eye out for any pests and diseases that may attack your plants now.

Rambler Roses

Most rambler roses will have done with flowering. If they are the type that produce long arching canes, cut back all older stems right to the base now. If the growth is congested, making them difficult to access, cut them back in short sections, then remove the pieces individually from among the other stems. New canes should be appearing from the base of the plant. Tie these in while they are still flexible. After pruning, feed the plants well with a rose fertilizer, water and mulch.

Top Tip

Some varieties of rose are more prone to black spot than others. If one of your plants is particularly badly affected, it may be best to dig it up and replace it with one that is known to be disease-resistant.

136

Rambler or Climber?

Many gardeners are puzzled by the distinction between rambler and climbing roses. Actually, the difference is not particularly clear cut, but as a general rule:

Ramblers

▶ Have a single, spectacular flush of flowers early in the season.

▶ The flowers are often small but carried in generous clusters.

▶ Growth is usually vigorous, with lots of new stems appearing near the base of the plant every year.

Climbers

▶ Either produce two separate flushes or flower intermittently over a long period from mid-summer into autumn.

▶ The flowers can be large, like those of a hybrid tea or floribunda.

▶ They produce new shoots from an established framework of stems, with only a few new shoots from the base every year.

Black Spot

Roses can be prone to black spot, a fungal disease that affects leaves and stems. If you notice large, circular black spots on the leaves, cut back all affected growth. Spray the rose with a fungicide, then feed and water well. The diseased material should be burnt, not composted, as the composting process does not destroy the fungal spores. Pick up and burn all shed leaves from around the base of the plants; spores on the ground can affect plants in the following year. It might be wise to replace the plant with a disease-resistant variety

Dahlias

If you keep picking the flowers for the house, the plants will carry on producing (albeit on short stems). Unlike other flowers, which can be picked in bud, dahlia flowers should be fully open when you pick them.

Earwigs

These large brownish-black insects often cause damage to open dahlia flowers (and also to late clematis), biting large holes in the petals and completely spoiling the appearance of the flowers. You can set traps for them as follows:

▶ Pack a small flower pot with straw.

▶ Invert the pot on a cane driven into the soil next to the affected plant.

▶ Empty the pot each morning and dispose of any earwigs that may be sheltering there.

Alliums

Alliums – or ornamental onions – are grown mainly for their spheres of flowers in late spring or summer. But the seedheads, which are ripening now, are almost as attractive, with their

geometric precision. It is worth collecting the seed from the heads as it ripens. Not only are alliums easily grown from seed, but this is much the best way to build up your stocks, as the bulbs are usually so expensive to buy.

▶ **Dry:** To harvest the seed, wait until the heads turn light brown and dry. The individual seed cases should just be starting to split.

▶ **Remove:** Cut stems from the plant.

▶ **Collect:** Shake the seedhead into a paper bag to release the seeds. Alternatively, suspend the stem upside down in a dry, warm place over a sheet of paper to catch the seeds as the cases continue to split.

Note: Seeds can be stored dry in paper bags or envelopes and kept in the refrigerator. Be sure to label the bags – many seeds look very similar.

Sweet Peas

Keep cutting flowers for the house and remove any seed pods you see. This will keep the plants productive. Also cut off any tendrils – these take energy from the plant. You may wish to leave a few seed pods on the plant to ripen if you want to collect seed for sowing later on.

Plants in Containers

All containers should be watered frequently during periods of hot weather. To cut down on water use, stand all the pots close together in a shady position. Not only will you waste less water, but you will also create a humid atmosphere among them that will help lower the temperature. If you are away on holiday, this will also help any friend or neighbour who is doing the watering for you. The plants may even survive a few days without watering.

Dead-Heading

Gardeners are frequently advised to dead-head plants. Removing spent flowers can either – in the case of roses and annuals – encourage the plant to carry on flowering, or – for spring shrubs – encourage fresh stems that will flower the following year. You are diverting the plant's energies away from seed production. But, in some instances, you may want to allow the plant to set seed, either because the seed cases or fruits are attractive, or because you want to collect the seed for use next year, so your dead-heading at this time of year should be selective. Plants with attractive hips or seed cases include:

▶ *Agapanthus* (seed cases)
▶ *Allium* (seed cases)
▶ *Eucomis bicolor* (seed cases)
▶ Ground-cover rose varieties with single
    flowers (hips)
▶ *Lunaria annua* (seed cases)
▶ *Nectaroscordum siculum* (seed cases)
▶ *Rosa glauca* (hips)
▶ *Rosa rugosa* (hips)

Rosa rugosa (Japanese rose, Ramanus rose) hips

Top Tip

It's worth allowing many annuals, especially sweet peas (*Lathyrus odoratus*), to develop a few seed cases, so that you can extract the seed later on.

Weeding

Keep on top of your weeding during this period. Weeds often harbour fungal diseases such as grey mould (*Botrytis*), which can then easily spread to ornamental plants.

Recycled Garden Waste

Many councils now sell bags of compost generated from green garden waste that is collected alongside general household waste. Unfortunately, it is not possible to guarantee the quality of this material. Although heat-treated, the compost may still contain weed seeds and traces of plant diseases. While it is unsuitable for use in containers or for sowing seed, it is excellent used as a mulch around utility plants such as trees and hedges.

Gardening Under Cover

At this time of year, you need to make sure that the plants in your greenhouse are kept cool. If it's hot outside, it can get doubly so near glass, which amplifies the heat.

Cuttings

Any softwood cuttings of plants that you took earlier in the season may be starting to root now. To test for rooting, give each cutting a gentle tug. If you feel resistance, the cutting has rooted. You will now have to pot on the cuttings, as follows:

▶ **New pot:** Pot each cutting up separately in a small pot of potting compost.

▶ **Harden off:** Stand the cuttings outdoors for increasing periods of time to harden them off.

▶ **Aftercare:** Water and feed the plants well.

Note: If the plants put on good growth between now and autumn, you may need to pot them on into slightly larger pots before the winter.

Fuchsia

Rooting Cuttings in Water

Cuttings of several soft-stemmed plants will root successfully in water if taken now. Cut short lengths of non-flowering shoots and strip off the lower leaves. Fill small tumblers or jars with water. Suspend the stems on a small piece of chicken wire or a few cocktail sticks so that the lower part of the stem (but not the leaves) trails in the water. Place the cuttings on a windowsill, but not in direct sunlight (which will scorch them). Change the water periodically so that it does not go green. The cuttings should root readily. Once they have developed a good root system, pot them up individually in multi-purpose compost. Suitable plants for this treatment include:

▶ *Diascia*
▶ *Impatiens* (busy Lizzie, indoor varieties)
▶ *Felicia* (swan river daisy)
▶ *Fuchsia*
▶ *Mentha* (mint)
▶ *Nemesia*
▶ *Osteospermum*
▶ *Penstemon*
▶ Tradescantia (wandering Jew)

Note: Roots produced in water tend to be very brittle and are easily broken, so take particular care when potting up the cuttings. Water them well so that they adapt quickly to the new growing medium

Tradescantia (wandering Jew)

Pelargoniums

Pelargoniums in the garden (and indoors) will carry on flowering, but this is a good time of year for planning ahead. If you take cuttings of your favourite plants now, they will be well rooted before winter and will provide you with plenty of material for use in containers and hanging baskets next year.

▶ **Pots:** Prepare pots or trays of multi-purpose compost mixed with equal parts sharp sand or grit.

▶ **Water:** Water the compost well and allow it to drain.

▶ **Cuttings:** Cut healthy, vigorous, non-flowering shoots from the plant. If the shoot tip is very soft, nip it out with finger and thumb, or snip with nail scissors.

▶ **Leaves:** Trim the cuttings at the base just below a leaf joint, then remove the lower leaves.

▶ **Compost:** Insert the cuttings into the compost so that the lowest leaf is just above the compost surface.

▶ **Position:** Keep the cuttings in a light position, but out of direct sunlight.

▶ **Pot on:** Once rooted, pot up the cuttings individually, using multi-purpose compost with added grit or sharp sand.

144

Cyclamen

Forms of *Cyclamen persicum*, which have flowers in white, pink and cherry red, are popular as flowering houseplants for the winter. If you have saved the tubers from last year (see p. 162), you can bring them back into growth now. You can bring cyclamen into growth as follows:

▶ **Clean:** Carefully remove the tuber from its pot and rub off the old compost.

▶ **Pot:** Using fresh potting compost, plant the tuber up in a pot of suitable size (just slightly wider than the tuber itself). Do not bury the tuber – the top should be just visible above the compost surface.

▶ **Position:** Place the pot in a light position but out of direct sunlight – around 16°C (61°F) is an ideal temperature.

▶ **Aftercare:** Water sparingly around (not on top of) the tuber, increasing the amount as it comes into growth.

Caring for Houseplants While on Holiday

Houseplants need regular watering during the summer months and can suffer from neglect if you are planning to be away from home for a period of weeks. Unless you have a friend or neighbour who will water the plants for you, you need to devise some method of preventing them from drying out. Some helpful tips for helping houseplants survive include:

▶ **Shade:** Group all the plants together in a shady spot (where water will evaporate more slowly).

▶ **Matting:** Stand them on capillary matting that can be thoroughly wetted before you go away.

▶ **Bowl:** Alternatively, place a bowl of water near the plants. Cut lengths of fabric tape and then bury one end of each in the compost of each container. Place the other ends of all the tapes in the water. The tapes will draw up the water by capillary action, preventing the compost from drying out completely.

Testing moisture levels

The Greenhouse

Keep the greenhouse cool by opening vents and doors whenever possible. Hose down the floor daily in dry weather. Keep turning plants so that they have equal access to the light on all sides. Make sure that leaves do not touch the glass – not only can they scorch, but beads of moisture (which can harbour fungal and bacterial diseases) will condense on them. Regularly scout the greenhouse for all signs of dead and decaying leaves – remove them from the environment and burn them.

Tomatoes

If you are growing your tomato plants on cordons, they have probably reached their desired height by now. To prevent further upright growth, pinch out the tip of the main shoot two leaves above the highest fruit truss.

Vine Weevil

Vine weevil is one of the worst greenhouse pests. The adult is a blackish insect that is active at this time of year. Vine weevils cannot fly, but they are excellent climbers. They clamber up the outside of the greenhouse and then drop through open vents and windows. They locate plants in containers, particularly cyclamen and begonias, and lay their eggs on the compost surface. The adults actually cause little damage themselves, apart from eating notches in leaves. But their larvae tunnel down into compost and eat plant roots and tubers over winter – you may not realize you have a problem until the following spring when pot plants suddenly fail to grow. Check plants regularly for signs of eaten leaves. If you suspect you have the weevil, kill the grubs by watering the containers with a parasitic nematode.

Dealing with Vine Weevil

When repotting plants at this time of year, check the roots carefully for vine weevil larvae (they are C-shaped and creamy white). If you spot any, wash the roots thoroughly (also to rid them of any unhatched eggs), then repot them in clean containers using fresh compost.

147

The Kitchen Garden

This is the start of the harvest season in many gardens. In some areas, the cooler nights may already bring a hint of autumn, as overnight dews become heavier.

New Sowings

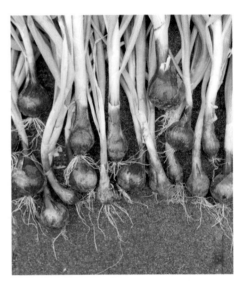

Make late sowings of quick-growing salad crops such as rocket and cut-and-come-again lettuces. Be sure to keep them in a cool position, however, as the seedlings may bolt.

Onions

As the foliage on onion plants starts to wither, onions can be lifted. Wait for a spell of warm weather so that the onions can ripen and harden for a few days in the sun – this is important if they are not to rot in storage. To lift onions, follow these simple steps:

▶ Sun: Bend over the stems and leaves to expose the bulbs to the sun.

▶ Lift: When the foliage has dried out and is straw-coloured, lift the onion bulbs from the soil.

▶ **Rest:** Leave the onions on the soil surface for a few days (cover them with a piece of chicken wire to deter pests). If you can raise the onions above the soil, so much the better. Try stretching a short length of chicken wire across two piles of bricks, and then placing the bulbs on the mesh to dry out.

Fruit

This is the start of the tree-fruit season in most gardens. The soft-season fruit is more or less over by now, though you may still have strawberries for picking, with autumn raspberries still to come.

Apples

Fruits of some varieties are ready to pick now. Cup a fruit in your hand and give it a gentle twist. It should come away with the stalk intact. Gather up and compost any windfall apples from around the base of trees. Large windfalls may be suitable for cooking (on dessert varieties, the fruit may not be ripe enough for eating raw).

Plums

Most plum varieties are ready for picking in late summer. They are ripe when the fruit parts easily from the stalk. Plums are best used straight from the tree, as they do not store well.

Morello Cherries

Morello cherries differ from nearly all other fruits in that they can be grown successfully in a shady situation. In these cooler conditions, the fruits (which are acid or sour in flavour) ripen somewhat later than sweet cherries. Pick them now for use in cooking and for preserves.

149

Herbs

A herb garden remains productive throughout this season.
Keep harvesting leaves from annual herbs such as parsley and
basil to prevent them running to seed – this process usually
toughens the leaves, impairing the flavour.

Making a Herb Hedge from Cuttings

Woody herbs such as rosemary (*Rosmarinus*), lavender
(*Lavandula*) and santolina are easily raised from cuttings taken at
this time of year. Just a few plants will provide enough material for
raising a whole hedge. To grow a herb hedge, you will need to:

▶ **Select shoots:** Find short, sturdy, non-flowering shoots on the plant (about 10–15 cm/4–6 in in length)
and snip them off, cutting just above a leaf joint.

▶ **Prepare:** Trim each cutting just below a leaf joint. Strip off the leaves from the lower half of each
cutting. You can usually do this easily just with finger and thumb.

▶ **Ground:** Insert the cuttings in the open ground, about 15 cm (6 in) apart. The lowest leaves should
be just above soil level.

▶ **Soil:** Water the cuttings well, and keep watering in the coming weeks so that the soil does not
dry out.

▶ **Replace:** The majority of the cuttings should root easily. Pull up any that fail and replace them with
ones that have rooted. Green-fingered gardeners sometimes make entire hedges *in situ*.

Plants To Enjoy

Trees

Aralia elata
   (Japanese angelica tree)

Genista aetnensis
   (Mount Etna broom)

Magnolia grandiflora (bull bay)

Hibiscus

Shrubs

Abelia

Abutilon

Buddleja davidii
   (butterfly bush)

Carpenteria

Ceanothus (California lilac)

Ceratostigma

Clerodendrum

Colutea

Cotinus (smoke bush)

Escallonia

Fuchsia

Hebe

Hibiscus

Hypericum (rose of Sharon)

Hyssopus (hyssop)

Itea

Lavandula (lavender)

Lavatera

Myrtus (myrtle)

Perovskia (Russian sage)

Phygelius

Potentilla

Rosa (rose)

Rosmarinus (rosemary)

Santolina (cotton lavender)

Spiraea

Yucca

151

Climbers

Actinidia kolomikta

Clematis

Eccremocarpus scaber (Chilean glory vine)

Humulus lupulus 'Aureus' (golden-leaved hop)

Ipomoea (morning glory)

Lathyrus grandiflorus (everlasting pea)

Lonicera (honeysuckle)

Passiflora (passion flower)

Polygonum (Russian vine)

Rosa (rose)

Solanum jasminoides 'Album'

Trachelospermum jasminoides (star jasmine)

Agapanthus

Perennials

Agapanthus

Alstroemeria (Peruvian lily)

Gypsophila (baby's breath)

Hosta

Nemesia

Osteospermum

Rudbeckia

Sedum (stonecrop)

Solidago (golden rod)

Verbascum

Verbena

Bulbs

Begonia

Crocosmia

Dahlia

Gladiolus

Lilium (lily)

Annuals and biennials

Ageratum (floss flower)

Alyssum

Eschscholzia

Godetia

Helianthus (sunflower)

Hosta

Lavatera

Lobelia

Matthiola (stock)

Mesembryanthemum (Livingstone daisy)

Nicotiana (tobacco plant)

Nigella (love in a mist)

Petunia

Salvia

Tagetes (African marigold, French marigold)

Tropaeolum (nasturtium)

Checklist

▶ **Hedges:** Give hedges their second cut of the year. Burn or shred the prunings.

▶ **Climbers:** Tie in the new growth of all climbers. Shorten any overlong stems. Prune rambler roses.

▶ **Cuttings:** Gradually harden off cuttings taken during spring and the early part of summer. Take cuttings of soft-stemmed tender perennials and other similar plants for rooting in water.

▶ **Earwigs:** Control these pests that may now be eating into dahlia and clematis flowers, among others.

▶ **Frogs and toads:** Make a cool place to shelter these amphibians during hot, dry periods – a pile of rocks or slabs, or just a patch of unmown grass, is usually sufficient.

▶ **Cyclamen:** Bring resting tubers of winter-flowering cyclamen back into growth. Keep them in good light and water sparingly around the tuber (not directly over it) initially.

▶ **Vine weevil:** Look out for signs of damage on the leaves of plants, especially those growing in containers. Water the containers using a parasitic nematode to kill the grubs before they can do any serious damage.

▶ **Onions:** Harvest onions as the foliage starts to wither.

▶ **Leafy vegetables:** Make late sowings of quick-growing salad crops. Keep them in a cool position.

▶ **Fruit:** Pick plums, cherries, peaches and other ripe tree fruits.

Early
Autumn

The Flower Garden

This can be a deceptive time of year. Sunny days make you think that it's still summer, while a cool night can remind you that winter is coming. Either way, it is an ideal time for getting a few things straight in the garden.

Lawns

Most lawns see heavy use in the summer, so you now have a good opportunity to spruce them up before winter so that they will provide the ideal recreation space next year. Since the rate of regrowth is starting to slow down at this time of year, reduce the frequency of your mowing. You should also endeavour to give your lawn the following treatments:

▶ **Remove:** Rake the lawn all over with a lawn rake. This important – though back-breaking – task fetches up all the accumulated dead growth ('thatch') from around the base of each blade of grass, much improving future growth.

▶ **Drainage:** Spike the lawn all over with a garden fork or special lawn slitter. The holes will improve the drainage of the lawn.

▶ **Top-dress:** Brush a mix of lawn sand and garden compost all over the lawn.

▶ **Feed:** Give the lawn a final feed before winter.

Feeding the lawn using a drop spreader to distribute the fertilizer

156

Repairing Damage

Lawns sometimes develop mounds and hollows, bare patches and ragged edges through general wear and tear. Now is the best time to tackle these problems, as there is plenty of time for the lawn to recover before next year.

▶ **Mounds:** Cut a cross across the mound with a sharp, long-bladed knife (an old kitchen knife is ideal), then peel back the turf. Scoop out excess soil to lower the mound, then fold back the turf.

▶ **Dips:** Cut a cross as for 'Mounds', and then raise the level of the soil underneath by adding a mix of good garden soil and sharp sand. Fold back the turf.

▶ **Bare patches:** Fork over the area with a hand fork. Remove some of the compacted soil with a trowel and replace with a mix of good garden soil and sharp sand. Sprinkle grass seed over and then water well.

▶ **Ragged edges:** With a half-moon cutter, cut a rectangle of turf from the edge of the lawn, around the ragged edge. Turn this around (a full 180°), so that the straight edge is flush with the edge of the lawn, with the jagged edge facing inwards. Sprinkle grass seed over the bare patch as for 'Bare Patches'.

Note: Turf usually knits back together very readily. Water over any repairs in the coming weeks if the weather stays dry.

157

Paving and Decking

With the weather turning increasingly damp at this time of year, a greenish film of algal growth often appears on decks, paths and patios. Not only is this unsightly, but it's slippery and it's all too easy to lose your footing on it. Treat all surfaces with an algicide during this period.

Did You Know?

The presence of moss – whether on a path, patio, deck or lawn, or in flower beds – always indicates a drainage problem. It's particularly likely to grow in dank, shady areas where any water that collects will be slow to evaporate.

Moss on lawns

While moss on lawns is easily treated with a moss-killer, the problem will recur unless you improve the drainage.

▶ **Treat:** First water a moss-killer over the moss. Within a few weeks, this will turn brown and start to die back.

▶ **Remove:** Rake the moss off with a lawn or scarifying rake.

▶ **Re-seed:** Fork over the bare patches and then sprinkle grass seed over.

Fuchsias

Fuchsias are invaluable garden plants, tolerant of some shade and with a long season of flowering. Many will still be going strong. Though they are often used as bedding plants, they are actually shrubs that can have a good life expectancy.

Hardy Fuchsias

Hardy fuchsias can overwinter successfully outdoors, given appropriate treatment:

▶ **Feed:** Give hardy fuchsias, whether they are in the garden or in containers, a dose of potassium now – a tomato fertilizer is ideal. This hardens the growth and protects it against winter frosts.

▶ **Sun:** If the plants are in containers, stand them in full sun on sunny days. This also toughens the stems and helps them withstand frost.

▶ **Mulch:** Apply a dry mulch in a doughnut-like ring around individual plants growing in the ground to protect the crown.

▶ **Protect:** As the nights turn colder, move fuchsias in containers into a sheltered position – a cold frame or porch is ideal.

159

Tender Fuchsias

If you garden in a frost-prone area, these plants will not survive the winter unprotected. To protect tender fuchsias:

▶ **Pot:** Lift fuchsias used in bedding schemes (or as a part of large container planting or hanging basket), shake the roots free of soil or potting compost, and pot up individually using fresh compost.

▶ **Sun:** Move the plants into a sunny position to ripen the stems (do not worry if the leaves shrivel and drop off).

A healthy fuchsia seedling

New penstemon plants are easy to raise from cuttings

▶ **Position:** Before the first frosts, transfer the fuchsias to a light, cool, but frost-free environment, such as a spare bedroom or porch.

▶ **Aftercare:** Water them sparingly once they have lost their leaves, just enough to stop the compost from drying out completely.

Tender Perennials

These stalwarts of summer bedding schemes, containers and hanging baskets are finally coming to the end of their flowering season. While it's possible to overwinter the plants by digging them up and potting them up, they may be exhausted after many months producing flowers. It's better to take cuttings and overwinter these for use next year, discarding the old parent plants.

Did You Know?

Shorter days and cooler nights persuade many plants that it's actually spring. Many spring-flowering shrubs and perennials will push out a few flowers at this time of year – before a really cold spell drives them into winter dormancy.

▶ **Shoots:** Find healthy, non-flowering shoots about 10 cm (4 in) long and snip these off with a pair of scissors or secateurs.

▶ **Leaves:** Strip off the leaves from the lower half of the stem with a sharp knife or finger and thumb.

▶ **Cuttings:** Pot up the cuttings in a mix of multi-purpose compost and sharp sand.

▶ **Warmth:** Tent the cuttings with a clear plastic bag and keep in a warm, light place (but out of direct sunlight).

▶ **Water:** Remove the bag and water regularly to keep the compost just moist.

▶ **Pot up:** When the cuttings are all well rooted, pot them up individually and keep them under cover until next summer.

Did You Know?

Large-leaved hebes (pictured right) are much less hardy than small-leaved ones (sometimes called 'whipcord' hebes). Take some cuttings now to be sure of having replacement plants should a hard winter kill a precious specimen.

Note:
Penstemons
– not reliably
hardy in all gardens –
can be raised from cuttings
in the same way, as an insurance
against possible winter losses.

161

Bulbs

Spring bulbs will start to appear in shops and garden centres. If you want particular varieties, buy online from specialist bulb suppliers. Bulk orders are usually the most economical way of buying. Large sacks of mixed bulbs are temptingly cheap. These are excellent for naturalizing in grass or for filling large containers. (For more on bulb planting, see p. 187.)

Tuberous Begonias

If you've used tuberous begonias in containers and hanging baskets, although they may appear to be dying, they can be stored for re-use next summer and do not have to be discarded.

▶ **Tubers:** Taking care not to damage them, lift the tubers carefully from the compost with a trowel or hand fork.

▶ **Sun:** Place the tubers in a sunny position and allow the remaining foliage to wither and start to die back.

▶ **Foliage:** Cut away the foliage and shake off the soil from around the roots.

▶ **Dry:** Allow the tubers to dry out for a further week in the sun.

▶ **Store:** Dust the tubers with a powdered fungicide and then store them in a cool, dry, dark place, ideally not touching.

Note: If the begonias have been grown in individual containers, simply stop watering, snip off the foliage after it has died back, and store the tubers in the containers in a cool, dark, dry place over winter.

Annuals

Pull up all spent annuals and add them to the compost heap (unless they show signs of disease). If plants are still flowering, encourage them to go on doing so for as long as possible by continuing to dead-head and water during dry spells. If you have devoted large areas to annuals, the soil may now be exhausted. After clearing the ground, fork in a general garden fertilizer (such as pelleted chicken manure) and a soil improver such as garden compost or well-rotted farmyard manure.

Note: If you made a late sowing of annuals in early summer and put out the plants in late summer, you can expect them to go on flowering until the first really hard frost.

Sow Now for an Early Display

It may seem strange, but you can actually sow hardy annuals now for early flowers next year. The seeds will germinate readily. Because you will need to protect the young plants during the worst of the winter, it's easiest to sow the seeds in rows in spare plots of ground (possibly in the vegetable garden) for transplanting in early spring. You can then cover them with a cloche or length of horticultural fleece on cold nights. Alternatively, raise them in small pots kept in a cold frame or unheated greenhouse over winter.

163

Spring bedding

You can replace summer annuals with hardy bedding plants that flower in spring. These are sometimes combined with spring bulbs, and can be planted at the same time. They can also be used (with or without bulbs) in large containers. Choose from:

- *Bellis perennis* (daisy)
- *Dianthus barbatus* (sweet William)
- *Erysimum cheiri* (wallflower)
- *Myosotis* (forget-me-not)
- *Primula*, Polyanthus group (polyanthus)

Dianthus barbatus (sweet William)

Myosotis (forget-me-not)

Note: Wallflowers belong to the same family as cabbages and are susceptible to certain diseases in the soil. It's best not to grow them in the same patch of ground each year, as the disease can build up and ruin the plants.

Gardening Under Cover

If you have a greenhouse, you will start to use it less for growing plants and more as a storage area. In the house, you will need to prepare plants for the coming winter.

Houseplants

If your houseplants spent the summer outdoors, bring them back inside now that the nights are getting cooler. Cut off any damaged leaves and give the pots a wipe down with a household detergent. Inspect the plants carefully, particularly the undersides of the leaves and the base of the pot – small slugs and other pests may be sheltering there. Flick off any you see or treat with a pesticide.

Preparing for Winter

Most houseplants are tropical or subtropical – in their country of origin they can be more or less permanently in growth, resting during dry periods. In temperate areas, it's usually best to induce a state of dormancy over the cooler months – most plants readily adapt to an enforced annual rest.

165

Stop feeding plants and reduce the rate at which you water them – in most cases, all you need do is water just enough to prevent the compost from drying out completely. Keep the plants in a light position, near a window, but be sure that they are not too close to the glass on cold nights, as a sudden drop in temperature can kill them.

Note: Cacti – which originate in desert regions – can be allowed to dry out completely in winter. But be prepared to give them a drink if they start to look a bit shrivelled.

Cymbidiums

If you grow cymbidium orchids, it is beneficial to keep them outdoors at this time of year. The steeply fluctuating temperatures between night and day actually encourage flower production. Place them in a sheltered spot, perhaps by the house wall or at the base of a deciduous tree. However, the plants are not hardy, so be sure to bring them back indoors should any early overnight frost be forecast.

Citrus

If you grow citrus trees (lemons, oranges, limes and various hybrids), make sure that they are not subjected to a sudden drop in temperature. If the plants are normally near glass, either move them well away from this on cold nights or make sure that they are near a heat source that keeps the temperature above 5°C (41°F).

166

In the Greenhouse

With the shortening days, most plants will benefit from maximum light if they are to carry on performing well. Remove all shading fabric attached to the roof. Shading washes on the sides of the house can normally be rubbed off with a damp cloth.

Grapes

Fruits on grapevines should be swelling nicely now. Harvest them by cutting whole trusses from the plant with long-bladed scissors.

Top Tip

If you have a heated greenhouse, check that whatever heating system you are using is in good working order now, well before the onset of winter.

167

The Kitchen Garden

This is the season of plenty in the garden, with quantities of beans, tomatoes and leafy vegetables to enjoy, alongside the first of the major root crops. Many tree fruits are also ripening now.

Root Vegetables

Lift beetroot, carrots and turnips and remove the leafy top-growth. They will store well if carefully dried off first. Rub or shake off excess soil, then allow them to dry in the sun for a couple of days to thicken the outer skins. Leave them unwashed. Store them in a cool, dark place, such as a shed or garage, loosely packed in straw. Small quantities can be bagged up and kept in the refrigerator. If you garden in a mild area where frosts are rare, and the soil is well-drained, you can leave the crops in the ground for harvesting as you need them.

Note: Only unblemished roots are suitable for storage.

Top Tip

Rather than cutting the leaves off beetroot, twist them off in your hand. A sharp cut can make the stems 'bleed' a purple juice.

Brussels Sprouts

On a windy site, stake the tall stems of Brussels sprouts so that they do not blow over in strong gales.

Green Manures

If you have a patch of ground that you have just cleared and that you are intending to

leave bare over winter, consider sowing a green manure instead. A green manure is a (usually) quick-growing plant that will help fix nitrogen in the soil, greatly improving the yields from future crops. As most grow as tight mats, they prevent weeds from germinating and also prevent soil erosion through autumn winds blowing across the soil surface, removing particles of valuable topsoil. The plants are allowed to

grow for two to three months, then dug into the soil, where they rapidly break down, leaving the ground ready to sow with an edible crop around four weeks later.

▶ **Soil:** Dig the soil over, removing any weeds as you do so, and then rake it level.

▶ **Sow:** Scatter the seeds over the soil surface. Lightly tap the surface with the back of a spade to ensure good adhesion between the seeds and the soil.

▶ **Water:** Water the seeded area well. The seeds should germinate within two to three weeks.

▶ **Patches:** Sow more seeds to fill any bare patches.

169

Note: Some green manures can be used in the longer term. Some clovers can be allowed to grow for a year – the flowers will attract bees and other pollinating insects.

Top Tip

If green-manure plants start to flower, snip them off and then dig the plants into the soil.

Tomatoes

Outdoor tomatoes will still probably have plenty of fruits on them, many of which will be green. Although you can pick them green and ripen them indoors, the best flavour develops if they can be left on the plants, which will need sheltering from the worst of the weather.

Green Manure Plants

Mustard

Crimson clover

Grazing rye

Winter tares

Winter field beans

Crimson clover

▶ **Straw:** Spread a layer of straw around the base of each plant.

▶ **Stems:** Gently bend the main stems down and rest them on the straw.

▶ **Protect:** Cover the plant with a glass or Perspex cloche or tunnel, open at each end. While allowing for good air circulation, this will warm the air around the fruits and also protect them from frost.

Did You Know?

Tomatoes – along with potatoes and aubergines – belong to the nightshade family, which includes many poisonous plants. Green fruits should never be eaten raw, but can be cooked in chutneys and pickles.

Apples

Many apple varieties will start to ripen now. Also, gather up any windfalls. They should be used immediately, after you have cut out any blemishes.

Storing Apples

While some varieties are best eaten straight from the tree, others store successfully – some for several months. In some cases, the flavour improves in storage as certain sugars develop and the texture of the flesh changes subtly, often becoming more mealy and less crisp.

Top Tip

Leave a few windfall apples around the base of the tree. They will feed foraging birds and beneficial wasps.

Store apples for a few weeks in clear plastic food bags in which you have pierced a few holes. Put the bags in the refrigerator and use as required. For longer-term storage, apples should be kept at around 0°C (32°F) in a well-ventilated place – a cold shed or garage is ideal. Some humidity prevents the fruits from shrivelling. Any doors must be kept securely closed, however, as the fruits will inevitably attract mice and rats over winter. To store apples successfully, follow this simple procedure:

Apples That Store Well

Belle de Boskoop

Egremont Russet

Granny Smith

Rhode Island Greening

Tydeman's Late Orange

172

▶ **Paper:** Wrap fruits individually in squares of silicone paper or baking parchment.

▶ **Crates:** Place the fruits in wooden or plastic crates. For good air circulation, the sides of the crates should have slots or holes in them.

▶ **Store:** Label the crates with the name of the variety and the date of picking, and stack them up.

Note: Apples for storage must be blemish free, or they will quickly rot.

Figs

Harvest figs only when they are fully ripe. Gently twist a fruit in your hands so that it comes away with its stalk intact. Ripe figs should be eaten as soon after picking as possible, but can be stored for a few days in the refrigerator.

Blueberries

Blueberries are ripe when the fruits have developed a whitish bloom. The leaves will probably be turning bright red at the same time.

Strawberries

Make new plantings of strawberries. Look for virus-free stock. If you are replacing existing strawberry plants, make a new bed in a different part of the garden to prevent a build-up of pests and diseases.

Raspberries

Harvest autumn raspberries now, either for eating fresh, freezing or jam-making. Leave the fruited canes unpruned over winter.

Blackberries and Hybrid Berries

Rubus idaeus x fruticosus (tayberries)

Harvest the fruits of blackberries and related fruits. Cut back the stems that have fruited this year. Stems produced during the current year will flower and fruit next year. If the plants have been trained on horizontal wires, weave the new stems into the support.

Did You Know?

Loganberries, tayberries and boysenberries are complex hybrids between blackberries and raspberries. They were bred to crop successfully in cool, damp climates where other fruiting plants that need sun are often disappointing.

Plants To Enjoy

Trees

Aralia elata
  (Japanese angelica tree)
Magnolia grandiflora
  (bull bay)
Malus
Metasequoia
Nyssa
Parrotia (ironwood)
Sorbus
Taxodium

Shrubs

Abelia
Buddleja davidii (butterfly bush)
Ceanothus (California lilac)
Ceratostigma
Chaenomeles
  (ornamental quince, japonica)
Clerodendrum
Cotoneaster
Escallonia
Euonymus

Sorbus (rowan tree, mountain ash)

Fuchsia
Hebe
Hibiscus
Hydrangea
Hypericum (rose of Sharon)
Hyssopus (hyssop)
Itea
Lavatera

Perovskia (Russian sage)
Phygelius
Potentilla
Pyracantha (firethorn)
Rosa (rose)
Rosmarinus (rosemary)
Viburnum
Yucca

175

Parthenocissus
(Virginia creeper, Boston ivy)

Climbers

Actinidia kolomikta
Akebia quinata
  (chocolate vine)
Ipomoea (morning glory)
Campsis radicans
Humulus lupulus 'Aureus'
  (golden-leaved hop)
Clematis

Parthenocissus (Virginia
  creeper, Boston ivy)
Passiflora (passion flower)
Polygonum (Russian vine)
Solanum jasminoides 'Album'
Vitis (vine)

Perennials

Aconitum (aconite)
Agapanthus
Anemone x hybrida
Aster (Michaelmas daisy)
Astilbe
Helenium
Hosta
Nemesia
Osteospermum
Pelargonium
Sedum (stonecrop)
Solidago (golden rod)
Verbena

Bulbs

Begonia
Colchicum (autumn crocus)
Dahlia
Gladiolus

Annuals and biennials

Ageratum (floss flower)
Alyssum
Helianthus (sunflower)
Lobelia
Matthiola (stock)
Mesembryanthemum
  (Livingstone daisy)
Nicotiana (tobacco plant)
Petunia
Tagetes (African marigold,
  French marigold)
Tropaeolum (nasturtium)

Ageratum (floss flower)

Checklist

▶ **Lawns:** Rake, spike and brush over a top-dressing. Repair worn areas. Treat any moss.

▶ **Fuchsias and tender perennials:** In cold districts, lift these plants for overwintering. Pot them up and take cuttings for use next year.

▶ **Bulbs and bedding:** Plant spring bulbs. Plant out spring bedding plants to replace annuals that have now finished flowering.

▶ **Annuals:** For early flowers next year, sow hardy annuals in pots or on patches of ground that can easily be protected with a cloche or fleece during the winter.

▶ **Greenhouses:** Remove all shading material and wipe off shading washes.

▶ **Root vegetables:** Lift fully grown beetroot, carrots and turnips, either for immediate use or for storage.

▶ **Green manures:** Sow a quick-growing green manure crop on areas of the vegetable garden that will not be used for edible crops again until next year.

▶ **Outdoor tomatoes:** Ripen the fruits by laying down the stems on a bed of straw placed next to each plant.

▶ **Fruit:** Harvest ripe fruit and prepare any excess for storage. Plant new strawberry plants (in a different patch of ground) as replacements for older plants that are no longer producing well. Cut back canes of blackberries and hyrbids that have fruited this year.

177

Mid-Autumn

The Flower Garden

There is usually a really cool feel to the days now, with the occasional reminder of summer. In fact, the weather is often spring-like at this time of year, enough to encourage you to get outdoors and get on top of some important jobs.

Trees and Shrubs

The leaves of many deciduous trees and shrubs will be turning rich yellow, red and orange now, before strong gales blow them off. Many others will be decorated with brightly coloured autumn fruits. Small wonder this is many people's favourite time of year.

Pyracantha

Key Trees and Shrubs

For good autumn leaf colour

Acer (maple)

Betula (birch)

Cotinus

Malus (crab apple)

Parrotia

Sorbus (rowan, mountain ash)

For decorative fruits and berries

Cotoneaster

Ilex (holly)

Malus (crab apple)

Pyracantha (firethorn)

Skimmia

Sorbus (rowan, mountain ash)

Making Leaf Mould

Leaf mould is the decomposed leaves of deciduous trees that has been allowed to break down over two to three years. It is one of the best soil improvers and is very easily made. Unlike composting (see p. 204), which relies on bacteria that generate heat, making leaf mould is a cold process, and the breakdown of the material is activated by fungi.

When ready, leaf mould makes an ideal growing medium, as it is high in plant nutrients, sweet-smelling and weed-free. Unlike garden compost (which contains bacteria and often carries weed seeds), it can be added to potting compost – particularly useful for growing woodland plants such as Japanese maples (forms of *Acer japonicum* and *A. palmatum*) and camellias.

To make leaf mould, collect fallen leaves in the autumn. They should be disease-free. Pack them loosely in black plastic sacks, pierce holes in the sides to allow for good air circulation and then put the sacks in a cool, dark place, such as a garage or cellar.

Leaf mould can also be made in the open air, though the leaves may be slower to break down, as the absence of light speeds up the decay. To make an outdoor heap:

▶ **Stakes:** Drive four stout stakes into the ground to form a square at least 1 m (3 ft) across.

▶ **Wire:** Wrap a length of chicken wire around the stakes and nail this in position to retain the leaves.

181

▶ **Leaves:** Pack the leaves loosely into this enclosure.

▶ **Turn:** Turn the heap periodically so that the leaves break down at an even rate. Note that it is not necessary to water the heap, as for a compost heap – the leaves dry out and crumble.

Planting

Autumn is the best time of year for planting deciduous trees and shrubs. All woody plants experience a surge in root growth at this time of year

and, although there may be nothing happening above ground until the following spring, roots can grow because the soil is still warm after the summer. This means that the plants will shoot vigorously when the next growing season arrives.

Note: Evergreens are slightly less hardy than deciduous plants, so are best planted in spring so they have a good six months to settle in before their first winter.

Bare-Root Plants

From now until early spring, bare-root plants are available and ready for planting. Many deciduous woody plants are sold bare-root and they are always much cheaper than container-grown plants. After unpacking the plants, cut back any stems that have been damaged in transit, cutting just above a dormant leaf bud. Shorten any overlong roots.

Prior to planting, soak the roots for at least an hour in a bucket of water. For 'Planting a container-grown tree or shrub', see p. 22. Plants often sold bare-root include:

- fruit trees and shrubs
- forest trees
- hedging plants
- roses

Heeling In

If you are unable to plant the bare-root plants straight away – because the ground is too dry, too wet or frozen, or if you just do not have the time – they can be 'heeled in' in a sheltered part of the garden until you are ready to do so. An empty bed in the vegetable garden is ideal.

- **Trench:** Roughly dig out a shallow trench about 30 cm (12 in) deep.

- **Soil:** Stand the plants in and then loosely spade the soil back over the roots. There is no need to firm them in. Heeling in is simply a means of preventing the roots from drying out before you have a chance to plant them properly.

Mycorrhizal Fungi

It's now widely believed that most trees and shrubs enjoy a symbiotic relationship with certain underground fungi. The fungi attach themselves to the roots and greatly increase the amount of water (and hence plant nutrients) that the plants can absorb. The fungi are sold packeted as a dry compound. Sprinkle this in at the base of the planting hole.

What is a Bare-Root Plant?

Unlike most of the plants on sale at garden centres – which have spent their entire lives in containers – bare-root plants have been grown in open fields at specialist nurseries. During the dormant season (autumn to winter), they are lifted from the ground and their roots are shaken free of soil. They are then loosely packaged up for sale. Dormant plants can survive well out of the ground. It is usually much more economical to buy plants this way (especially for bulk orders for hedging), as the nursery does not have to invest time and money in potting plants on annually, watering and feeding.

▶ **Plant:** When you are ready to plant them in their designated positions, simply fork them up and shake the soil from the roots.

Note: Most bare-root plants can be stored in their packaging (unopened) in a cool, dry place, such as a shed, for up to four weeks. They will come to no harm.

Semi-Ripe Cuttings

Many woody plants – trees, shrubs and climbers – are easily raised from cuttings taken at this time of year. Rooting can be quite slow, however – up to six months in some cases.

▶ **Stem:** Cut lengths of the current season's growth, about 15–20 cm (6–8 in) long. Take the cutting just above a leaf joint on the parent plant.

▶ **Cutting:** Trim each cutting at the base, just below the lowest leaf joint. Cut off the leaves from the lower half of each cutting to leave a bare length of stem.

▶ **Compost:** Insert the cuttings in pots or trays filled with cuttings compost (equal parts multi-purpose compost and sharp sand or grit).

▶ **Position:** Water the cuttings well. Put them in a sheltered place outdoors, ideally in a cold frame or unheated greenhouse.

▶ **Pot on:** When they are well rooted, pot the cuttings up into individual containers filled with potting compost.

184

▶ **Aftercare:** Most semi-ripe cuttings need little attention over the coming months. Water them to prevent the compost from drying out and remove any dead leaves that might rot and kill the cutting.

Note: Cuttings taken from deciduous plants will behave like the parents – in other words, they will lose their leaves as the days shorten and temperatures are lower. This is a normal process and does not indicate that the cutting is dead.

Perennials

While late-flowering perennials and grasses continue to provide interest in the flower garden, most others are starting to die back now. Cut back dead growth and mulch around plants to improve the soil for next year.

Dividing Perennials

Many perennials can be divided now, and this is an excellent opportunity to bring back under control any plants that have made excessive growth over the summer.

▶ **Stems:** Cut back any dead stems, if necessary.

▶ **Fork:** Dig up the plants using a garden fork (a hand fork may be suitable for smaller, low-growing plants).

Top Tip

When taking cuttings, always look for healthy, vigorous, undamaged stems – these will grow into the best plants.

> **Split:** Divide clumps into smaller pieces, with your hands, an old kitchen knife or two garden forks held back to back.

> **Plant:** Replant the best pieces. Older sections can either be chopped up and added to the compost heap or burnt.

Exotic Strangers

Musa basjoo (banana palm)

Architectural plants such as banana palms (*Musa basjoo*) and tree ferns (*Dicksonia antarctica*) have become popular garden plants, but are far from hardy. In many situations, they will not survive the winter unless given some protection now. Survival depends on sheltering the top growth from the worst ravages of winter.

> **Banana palms:** Wait until the first hard frost has blackened all the foliage, then cut or strip this off to leave a bare stem (larger specimens may have several stems). Encircle the stem or stems with a length of chicken wire and then pack this loosely with dry straw. The straw should reach above the tops of the stems. Cover the top with a plastic sheet to keep off the damp.

> **Tree ferns:** Place a collar of chicken wire around the trunk and loosely pack this with dry straw. Leave the fronds at the top of the stem to die back naturally. If the weather turns very cold, pack straw loosely over the top of the plant.

Note: The straw you use for insulation must be absolutely dry. Take care not to pack too tightly – the aim is to keep the plants dry over winter, so good air circulation through the material is essential.

Planting Bulbs

This is the main season for planting spring bulbs. They are often sold loose as bare bulbs or bagged up, packed in straw. It is always much cheaper to buy them this way than as flowering plants in containers in spring.

Note: Most bulbs are planted to twice their own depth. In other words, if a bulb measures 2.5 cm (1 in) from base to tip, dig a hole 7.5 cm (3 in) deep to allow for 5 cm (2 in) of soil above the bulb.

Naturalizing Bulbs in Lawns

Bulbs are always effective planted in drifts in lawns. For the most striking effect, choose quantities of the same variety. Note that the varieties you choose have to be vigorous enough to compete with the grass. For small bulbs, such as crocuses, simply remove squares of turf here and there. Place up to 10 bulbs on each patch of exposed soil, then ease the turf back into place. For larger bulbs, follow this sequence:

▶ **Bulbs:** Scatter the bulbs across the lawn.

▶ **Soil:** Dig out a plug of soil from the lawn of the appropriate depth where each one has landed. Use either a sturdy trowel or a special bulb-planting tool.

▶ **Plant:** Place a bulb at the base of the hole.

▶ **Lawn:** Replace the plug of soil and firm well to restore the level of the lawn.

Top Tip

Delay planting tulips until late autumn. Planted too early, they may start into growth prematurely and not flower properly.

187

Top Tip

If the ground you are planting is very hard, use a special bulb auger to help you dig holes of the appropriate size.

Note: If the bulbs are to flower successfully in future years, they have to be allowed to complete their growth cycle. Mowing the lawn has to be delayed until roughly four to six weeks after the bulbs have finished flowering and have started to die back.

If you have to mow the lawn, then simply mow round the clumps.

Bulbs in Containers

With bulbs being so cheap, you can afford to plan for bold, generous plantings in large containers next to the front door – you will be glad you did when they reward you with a brilliant display next spring.

▶ **Container:** Line the base of the container with crocks, large stones or chunks of polystyrene.

Early Bulbs for Planting in Lawns

Chionodoxa (glory of the snow)

Crocus (large-flowered hybrids)

Crocus tommasinianus

Fritillaria meleagris

Hyacinthoides non-scripta

(English bluebell)

Narcissus (dwarf types, daffodil)

Crocus

188

▶ **Compost:** Start to fill the container with potting compost (multi-purpose mixed with grit, sharp sand or perlite or vermiculite is ideal).

▶ **First layer:** Put in a layer of bulbs. For the boldest effect, set them as close together as you can without them touching. Add more compost to come halfway up the bulbs.

▶ **Second layer:** Put in another layer of bulbs, in the spaces between the first layer's 'noses'. Fill the container to within 1 cm (½ in) of the rim to allow for watering.

▶ **Top-dress:** Top with a layer of grit. (For added interest, sprinkle grass seed on the compost surface to create a mini lawn.)

Perlite (centre) and vermiculite (right)

189

Note: If the bulbs are tall varieties (30 cm/12 in or more), you could try pushing in lengths of willow or hazel around the edge of the pot and bending them over to form hoops. Not only are these very decorative, but they will also support the bulbs' stems as they develop early next year.

Some narcissus bulbs appear to have split into two, with two 'noses' (or growing points). Before planting, snap them apart and treat as two individual bulbs.

Storing Dahlias

Dahlias will be a spent force by now – though, if you have been picking the flowers regularly, the plants may still be productive. Assuming the plants have no more buds on them, prepare the tubers for winter:

▶ **Leaves:** When the leaves turn black, cut back the main stems to about 15 cm (6 in) above the ground.

▶ **Canes:** Remove any stakes or canes for reuse next year.

Top Tip

A planted container can be very heavy and difficult to move. Put the container in its final position before beginning to plant it up.

Did You Know?

A bulb is composed of modified leaves attached at the base to a thickened stubby stem. In growth, these leaves stretch upwards and turn green once they emerge from under ground.

▶ **Tubers:** Carefully lift the tubers from the ground.

▶ **Soil:** With your fingers, rub off as much soil from the tubers as you can. Dry off the tubers in an airy shed or unheated greenhouse.

▶ **Storage:** Store the tubers in paper bags in a cool, frost-free place such as a shed or garage. They may shrivel slightly over winter, but will spring back into productive life next year.

Note: If you garden in a mild area, it's possible to overwinter dahlias in the garden. Simply cut the stems back to ground level, then cover the plants with a layer of dry straw (or similar material) around 10 cm (4 in) deep. Cover the straw with a short length of chicken wire to stop it blowing away.

191

Sweet Peas

Sow seeds of sweet peas (*Lathyrus odoratus*) now for flowers the following summer. Plants raised from seed in autumn are sturdier and will come into flower earlier. However, the seeds have to be germinated in containers so that they can easily be protected from hard frosts, mice and slugs.

Sowing the Seed

Sow the seeds in 12.5 cm (5 in) pots or special containers made specifically for sweet peas and other plants that develop deep root systems. To sow sweet-pea seeds:

▶ **Soil:** Fill the containers with seed compost or multi-purpose compost.

▶ **Hole:** Make a hole about 1 cm (½ in) deep in the compost for each seed with a dibber or pencil.

▶ **Seeds:** Plant the seeds and then draw the surrounding compost over them.

▶ **Water:** Do not firm the compost, but lightly consolidate it by watering with a can fitted with a fine rose.

▶ **Position:** Place the containers in a sheltered place outdoors. Keep them in a cold frame during periods of freezing weather.

Gardening Under Cover

While indoor tomatoes and similar crops have mostly finished by now, you can make use of whatever space you can spare indoors for displays of flowers early next year.

The Greenhouse

Early bulbs outdoors can be ruined by sudden changes in the weather. An unheated greenhouse that is going to stand largely empty over the winter can be used for producing plants with perfect flowers.

▶ **Bulbs:** Pot up the bulbs in shallow pots or pans filled with gritty compost.

▶ **Greenhouse:** Keep all the vents of the greenhouse open, apart from on nights when freezing temperatures are expected.

Early Bulbs for an Unheated Greenhouse

Crocus

Iris danfordiae

Iris reticulata

Narcissus bulbocodium

193

Hyacinth

▶ **Flowers:** When the flower buds start to show colour, you can bring the pots into the house for interior decoration – or remember to visit the greenhouse daily to enjoy them.

Note: Start watering the pots in mid-winter to encourage the bulbs into growth.

Bulbs for Indoors

As well as hyacinths that have been specially treated to flower ahead of their natural season (*see* below), there are a number of other bulbs, usually deliciously scented, that flower early and are unsuitable for garden use because they do not stand up to harsh weather. These include Paperwhite and Soleil d'Or narcissi.

Narcissus shoots

Plant up the bulbs in containers about 25 cm (10 in) across. Insert a cane next to each bulb to which you can tie the stems as they begin to grow. Keep them in a cool but light position and then move them into the living room when the flower buds begin to open.

Forcing Hyacinths

Specially prepared hyacinth bulbs that will flower in the middle of winter should be planted now. The bulbs have been kept in controlled conditions that encourage them into early flowering.

Hyacinth shoots

194

▶ **Bowls:** Half-fill shallow bowls with bulb fibre.

▶ **Bulbs:** Lightly press the bulbs on to the compost surface. Feed more compost through your fingers around the bulbs. The 'noses' of the bulbs should be just sticking out above the compost surface.

▶ **Water:** Water gently to moisten the compost.

▶ **Storage:** Keep the bowls in a cool, dark place. Check them occasionally and water them just enough to keep the compost moist.

▶ **Light:** When the shoots are about 5 cm (2 in) high, bring the bowls out of the dark and place them in a light position (but out of direct sunlight). The bulbs will then continue to grow and flower.

Note: Hyacinth bulbs can also be grown in special glasses filled with water.

Top Tip

It is best not to plant hyacinth bulbs of different colours in the same container as these will rarely flower at the same time.

What is Bulb Fibre?

Bulb fibre is a growing medium that has been specially formulated for indoor bulbs. It contains pieces of charcoal (or similar material) to keep it sweet smelling. Bulb fibre can be used in shallow decorative containers without drainage holes.

The Kitchen Garden

If you have been busy in the kitchen garden all year, you will now enjoy a glow of satisfaction as you contemplate a winter's worth of produce you have grown yourself.

Potatoes

Dig up your main crop of potatoes now, before the worst of the weather. While it is usually safe to leave them in the ground for a while after the foliage has died down, they should be lifted before the first really hard frost. If you are lifting the whole crop for storage, choose a dry, sunny day.

▶ **Fork:** Lift the potatoes with a garden fork, taking care not to damage individual tubers (any that you do accidentally damage should be used straight away).

▶ **Dry:** Leave the tubers on the soil surface to dry out for a couple of hours. This toughens the outer skins.

▶ **Soil:** Lightly shake or brush off any soil clinging to the tubers.

▶ **Size:** Sort the potatoes by size. Small ones should be eaten as soon as possible, but large ones can be stored for use over the coming months.

▶ **Sacks:** Pile the larger potatoes into large sacks. Stout paper sacks are best, but you can also use black plastic bags provided you make a few slits in the sides for ventilation.

▶ **Storage:** Store the potatoes in a cool, dark, dry place such as a cellar, shed or garage.

Note: Potatoes are best stored unwashed.

Blanching Stem Vegetables

For white stems on celery and leeks, either wrap special collars around each plant or mound up the earth around them. Excluding light prevents them from producing green pigment and keeps the tissues tender.

Apples

Carry on picking the fruits from later-ripening varieties, for using fresh, for cooking or for storing (see p. 172). Collect fallen fruits and leaves from around the base of trees. Add these to the compost heap, or use the leaves for making leaf mould (see p. 181).

Winter Codling Moth

This is a common pest on apple trees, but it is easy to deal with if you take preventive action at this time of year. The female moths cannot fly, but climb up apple tree trunks to lay their eggs on tree branches, exactly where next year's flower buds will appear. The grubs then tunnel into the flowers and eat the developing fruit from the inside. The moth is easily deterred by wrapping a grease band around the trunk that stops the moths in their tracks. Simple, but effective.

197

Soft Fruits

While summer is the main season for soft fruits, devote some time to the plants themselves now, to be sure of healthy plants and good crops next year.

Raspberries
On summer-fruiting varieties, cut back to the ground all stems that have fruited. Stems produced this year will flower and fruit next year, so leave these unpruned.

Strawberries
If you grow late-fruiting varieties, protect the plants from the worst of the weather with a small tunnel cloche, which should be left open at both ends.

Herbs

If you made late sowings of annual herbs such as parsley and basil, you can keep them going for a few weeks longer by protecting them with cloches. The rigid, clear, plastic tunnel-type is the most suitable. Left open at each end, it will allow for good air circulation, while raising the temperature around the plants and keeping the worst of the season's weather off the plants.

Note: Keep harvesting leaves from parsley plants. If you allow them to flower, the leaves will toughen and the flavour will not be as good.

Plants To Enjoy

Trees

Acer (maple)

Amelanchier

Arbutus (strawberry tree)

Aralia elata
   (Japanese angelica tree)

Cornus kousa

Ginkgo

Malus (crab apple)

Metasequoia

Nyssa

Parrotia (ironwood)

Prunus (ornamental cherry)

Sorbus

Taxodium

Shrubs

Abelia

Berberis

Callicarpa

Berberis

Ceratostigma

Chaenomeles (ornamental
   quince)

Clerodendrum

Cotoneaster

Escallonia

Euonymus

Fuchsia

Hamamelis (witch hazel)

Hebe

Hibiscus

Hypericum (rose of Sharon)

Perovskia (Russian sage)

Amelanchier

199

Solidago (golden rod)

Potentilla
Pyracantha (firethorn)
Rosa (rose)
Skimmia
Viburnum

Climbers

Akebia quinata
  (chocolate vine)
Humulus lupulus 'Aureus'
  (golden-leaved hop)
Ipomoea (morning glory)

Parthenocissus
  (Virginia creeper,
  Boston ivy)
Solanum jasminoides 'Album'
Vitis (vine)

Perennials

Aster (Michaelmas daisy)
Gentiana (gentian)
Helenium
Rudbeckia
Schizostylis

Solidago (golden rod)
Verbena

Bulbs

Amaryllis belladonna
Dahlia
Nerine

Annuals and biennials

Antirrhinum (snapdragon)
Lobelia
Mesembryanthemum
  (Livingstone daisy)
Nicotiana (tobacco plant)
Petunia
Tagetes (African marigold,
  French marigold)

Helenium

200

Checklist

▶ **Leaf mould:** Make use of fallen leaves by turning them into leaf mould. Either build up a heap outdoors or bag them up for storing in a cool, dry place.

▶ **Trees and shrubs:** Plant bare-root plants – garden trees, fruit trees, deciduous hedges, roses and fruit bushes. Heel them in if conditions are unsuitable for immediate planting.

▶ **Cuttings:** Take semi-ripe cuttings of a range of shrubs and climbers.

▶ **Perennials:** Cut back and divide overgrown perennials.

▶ **Dahlias:** Lift dahlias after the topgrowth has been blackened by frost and dry off the tubers for storage.

▶ **Spring bulbs:** Plant these in beds or containers. If you have a greenhouse, pot up a few early-flowering ones for growing under glass. Plant up some forced hyacinth bulbs for mid-winter flowers indoors.

▶ **Protect over winter:** Large plants that may not be fully hardy, such as banana palms (*Musa*) and tree ferns (*Dicksonia*), should be packed with straw in areas where hard winters are anticipated.

▶ **Sweet peas:** For the best plants, sow seed now.

▶ **Potatoes:** Dig up and dry off maincrop potatoes for storing over the coming months.

▶ **Fruit:** Pick late-ripening apples. Protect trees against winter codling moth. Cut back to ground level all the fruited stems on summer-fruiting raspberry varieties.

Late Autumn

The Flower Garden

The garden is beginning to look bare now, but there are still a few late-flowering perennials, bulbs and grasses to add interest to the shortening days. New plantings, taking cuttings and sowing seed will keep you looking ahead.

Composting

With so much dead plant material around, this is a good time to make a compost heap if you don't already have one. Garden compost is the number one soil improver, as it is so high in plant nutrients. You can speed up the rate at which the composting material breaks down by adding a compost activator, either a compound sprinkled on between the layers or as a liquid. One of the best of all activators is also the most readily available – your own urine (and other people's). You can apply this direct from the source or first collected in a suitable receptacle. Either way – be discreet about it.

What Can I Compost?

All kinds of material of organic origin can be put on the heap. The ideal is a balanced mix of a range of different materials, including:

▶ Plant remains – dead leaves, flowers and stems
▶ Vegetable peelings from the kitchen
▶ Egg shells
▶ Grass mowings

204

- Cardboard and paper (best shredded)
- Any natural fibre (e.g. cotton, wool and silk)

Making the Heap

Although you can make compost in a large plastic bin, these are seldom wide enough. A compost heap should be at least 1 m (3 ft) wide in both directions so that the material within the heap is sufficiently insulated for the bacteria that break it down to become active.

You can make a simple heap with four stout stakes and chicken wire (see 'Making Leaf Mould', p. 181). Even better – because it is better insulated – is a timber construction with three solid sides and a fourth that can be removed for easy access to the compost. Ideally, you should turn the compost every couple of weeks with a garden fork so that the material breaks down at an even rate.

Using Poor Compost

If you already have a compost heap, but the result is cold, slimy and smelly, it can still be used. Simply spread the half-decayed material over bare beds and borders, on the vegetable garden or around established trees and shrubs (though it should not touch the bark). The material will carry on breaking down over winter and the earthworms will do some of the work for you, pulling it down underground. It will all have vanished by next spring, and the resulting soil will be sweet-smelling and workable.

What Not to Compost

Meat

Fish

Dairy products

Cooked vegetables

Seeds

Diseased plant material

Evergreen plants

Potato peelings

Trees and Shrubs

While most trees and shrubs are winding down for their winter rest, with bare branches making a tracery against the sky, others will be thronged with birds foraging for berries and invertebrate life sheltering in the bark.

Growing from Seed

Many trees and shrubs are surprisingly easy to grow from seed. You need to be patient, however, as germination can be slow. Some seed is encased in a fleshy berry – important for attracting birds, which eat the fruit and then release the seed in their droppings. It's easy to extract the seed for sowing, as described below:

▶ **Ripe:** Cut a few bunches of berries when they are soft and ripe – usually just after the first hard frost. Squash the berries to release the seeds.

▶ **Clean:** Wash the seeds in lukewarm water to remove any fruity flesh clinging to them. Dry the seeds on absorbent kitchen paper.

▶ **Compost:** Fill 7.5 cm (3 in) containers with multi-purpose or seed compost, water and allow to drain.

▶ **Seed:** Sow the seeds on the compost surface, two or three per container.

▶ **Top-dress:** Top the seeds with a layer of grit or sharp sand.

▶ **Position:** Place the containers outdoors. Exposure to harsh weather is actually beneficial. Alternatively, put the containers in the fridge for up to six weeks and then put them outdoors. Low temperatures break the seeds' dormancy, allowing them to germinate the following spring.

Cuttings

You can carry on taking cuttings of shrubs throughout late autumn. Depending on the firmness of the growth, treat them either as semi-ripe cuttings (see p. 184) or hardwood cuttings (see p. 226).

Note: Hardwood cuttings of deciduous plants are generally taken after leaf fall.

Trees and Shrubs in Containers

Permanent plants in containers are rather more vulnerable over winter than plants in the open ground, because their roots are not protected by a layer of soil. Loosely wrap the containers in a length of horticultural fleece or hessian, or simply stand the container in a slightly larger one – the insulation will prevent the roots from freezing on cold nights.

Camellias in Containers

These beautiful evergreen shrubs have special needs at this time of year if you are growing them in containers. Next year's flower buds are already starting to swell, and you need to keep the plants well watered, otherwise they will be shed just before opening in the spring. Water the plants freely on mild days so that the compost never dries out.

Trees and Shrubs with Fleshy Berries or Hips

Cotoneaster
Ilex (holly)
Pyracantha (firethorn)
Rosa rugosa
Skimmia
Sorbus (rowan, mountain ash)
Taxus (yew)

Sorbus (rowan, mountain ash)

207

Transplanting an Established Shrub

This is the best time of year for moving established evergreen shrubs and conifers. Prepare the new
site first. Fork over the soil and remove any large stones and any perennial weeds. Improve the soil as
necessary by forking in garden compost or another soil improver. Grit will help with drainage if the ground is
very heavy. Have ready a length of hessian or stout plastic sheeting to wrap the rootball in – both to prevent
excessive moisture loss from the roots and to make the plant easier to carry to its new home.

▶ **Hole:** Dig a large planting hole to match the spread of the plant's top growth.

▶ **Soil:** Loosen the soil at the base of the hole with a fork and incorporate more organic matter and/or grit.

▶ **Dig up:** Dig around the plant you want to move, cutting through its roots with the spade as you do so.
With the spade horizontal, cut underneath the shrub on all sides to sever the roots.

▶ **Lift out:** Remove the shrub carefully, with the soil still clinging to the roots. Place the rootball on the
hessian or plastic sheet.

▶ **Protect:** Wrap the sheet around the rootball and tie it loosely to the trunk or lower stems with tape or
garden twine.

▶ **Move:** Carry the plant to its new home. Remove the covering from around the roots and set the plant
in the middle of the hole.

▶ **Plant:** Check the planting depth with a cane or length of bamboo laid across the hole. Add more soil
to (or remove soil from) the base of the hole as necessary.

▶ **Backfill:** With the plant in position, backfill around the rootball with the excavated soil.

▶ **Aftercare:** Water the plant well and spread a mulch of organic matter in a doughnut-like ring around the lower stem or stems.

Note: When moving an established shrub or conifer, it's actually beneficial to cut through some of the thicker roots in order to lift it from its original position. Hair-like new roots will develop from around the cut surfaces, and these will be much more efficient at taking up moisture than the older ones, meaning that the plant will be able to grow away vigorously next spring.

Whenever you are moving a conifer, choose a mild, damp day. The needles are much less likely to dry out, a common cause of failure to thrive in the new planting position.

Root-balled Conifers

While it's usual to buy conifers as container-grown plants, they are sometimes sold at this time of year as 'root balled' – especially large yews for hedging. A root-balled conifer has been grown at a nursery in an open field. The plants are dug up shortly before sale, with the soil still clinging to the roots. The root ball is held in place with either a plastic or metal cage or a length of hessian. Either way, root-balled conifers should be planted straight away. Unlike bare-root plants (see p. 182), they will not survive for long unplanted. While they are generally robust and tough plants, they are actually quite vulnerable and resent being dug up – a sudden move can kill them ('transplant shock'). The cage or other covering should be removed just before planting.

Top Tip

Evergreen shrubs and conifers are heavy plants and can be unwieldy. If necessary, enlist the help of a fellow gardener when moving one.

Health and Safety

Conifer stems are often covered in sharp needles. When moving one, eye injuries are always a risk. Keep safe by wearing goggles and stout gloves.

209

Roses

It's not too late to order bare-root roses from rose growers and nurserymen. Check lead times for delivery and – ideally – plant them as soon as you are able to, weather permitting.

Pruning

Many roses, especially hybrid teas and floribundas, will have made a lot of growth over the previous months. This can make them susceptible to 'wind rock' (when gales almost pull the plants right out of the ground, exposing the graft union and the upper parts of the roots to the air). To lessen the risk of this, lightly prune back some of the stems to make a more compact plant.

Note: Pruning roses at this time of year can encourage them into premature growth that will be susceptible to frost damage. Cut them back only if they are particularly unbalanced and are sited in an exposed part of the garden. Roses in a sheltered position are best left unpruned over winter.

Climbers

Deciduous climbers will have made a lot of new growth over summer and may now be a mass of tangled stems. While major pruning is best left until after the worst of the winter weather, some can be tidied up now.

Humulus lupulus (Hop)

Pruning

Cut back loose, wayward stems of climbing hydrangea (*Hydrangea petiolaris*), *Pileostegia*, *Schizophragma* and Virginia creeper and Boston ivy (*Parthenocissus*), particularly from around windows and doorways. The golden-leaved hop (*Humulus lupulus* 'Aureus') will be looking very ragged by now. As it shoots freely from the base each year, you can safely prune it now. Cut the stems back to near ground level, then remove the dead stems from their support.

Perennials

Cut back dry foliage and stems of late-flowering perennials such as rudbeckias and Michaelmas daisies (*Aster*). Leave seedheads on sedums – they will feed birds in winter as well as protecting the crown of the plant against winter frosts. Seedheads can also be left on grasses, as they are often highly decorative.

Aster (spent Michaelmas daisies)

Top Tip

Leave the silky seedheads of clematis on the plants over winter. They turn fluffy during dry weather and the birds will use them early next year for lining their nests.

Tender Perennials

If you have decided to take a chance on leaving tender perennials such as penstemons and osteospermums in the ground over winter, protect them from the worst of the weather to come with a dry mulch. Straw packed loosely around the stems is an ideal material. A short piece of chicken wire bent over it will prevent it from blowing away.

211

Collecting Seed

Seed is ripening on many summer bulbs and perennials. While it's usual to cut off the seedheads to keep the plant vigorous, it's worth leaving a few for raising new plants. Not all plants can be grown from seed, however – only true species, not hybrids, will produce seed worth sowing. Seed is ripe when the seed cases turn brown and start to split. Ripe seed is usually (but not always) dark in colour. You can strip dry seed from grasses by pulling the stems through your fingers. Plants to grow from seed include:

- ▶ *Acanthus* (bear's breeches)
- ▶ *Agapanthus*
- ▶ *Alcea rosea* (hollyhock)
- ▶ *Allium* (ornamental onion)
- ▶ *Eucomis bicolor*
  (pineapple lily)
- ▶ *Grasses*
- ▶ *Hosta sieboldiana*
- ▶ *Iris sibirica*
- ▶ *Lilium regale*
  (regal lily)
- ▶ *Papaver orientale*
  (poppy)

Sowing seed

Once you have collected the seed you would like to sow, it can be sown in small pots, as follows:

▶ **Compost:** Fill 7.5 cm (3 in) pots with multi-purpose or seed compost.

▶ **Seed:** Sow the seed thinly on the surface (no more than five seeds, if you are able to sow them individually) and then top with a thin layer of compost followed by grit or sharp sand.

▶ **Position:** Stand the pots in a sheltered spot outdoors.
If they germinate straight away, put them in a cold frame to protect them from frost, and keep them there until the following spring. Otherwise, leave the pots outdoors, and the seedlings should appear in spring.

▶ **Aftercare:** Water the containers sparingly, just enough to keep the compost from drying out.

Did You Know?

'Winter' pansies are the same as ordinary pansies – but you can't grow them yourself from seed. Commercially, the seeds are sown in summer but kept at low temperatures – essential for the initial stages – that would be difficult to maintain at home.

Bedding Plants

You can continue to plant up bare areas with spring bedding plants (see p. 164) and, for earlier colour, winter pansies. Note that winter pansies do not flower throughout the cold months but intermittently during mild spells. Order seeds for next year's summer display. You will have a much better choice ordering from a seed company than buying over the counter in spring. Popular varieties often sell out quickly.

Plant a Winter Window Box

You may not want to venture far into the garden during the coming cold season, so why not bring the garden to the house? If you are short of time, instead of filling the box with potting compost, simply stand the plants in it still in their original containers – they will not grow much over winter. Fill in any gaps between with either compost or moss. Add some trailing ivys to soften the edge. Suitable plants for a winter window box include:

▶ Small berrying shrubs
(such as skimmias and pernettyas)

▶ Dwarf early-flowering bulbs
(such as daffodils,
crocuses and tulips)

▶ Dwarf conifers

▶ Heathers

▶ Cyclamen

Note: Any window
box should be securely
fastened to the sill.

214

Bulbs

Tulips (*Tulipa*) are best planted now. They combine well with spring bedding plants such as forget-me-nots (*Myosotis*) and wallflowers (*Erysimum*). You can also plant autumn-flowering nerines (*Nerine bowdenii*) if you have a suitable sheltered spot, such as at the base of a warm wall. Plant the bulbs 7.5–10 cm (3–4 in) apart in well-drained soil. Protect the new plantings with a mulch of dry straw (this should not be necessary in subsequent years).

Nerine bulb

Top Tip

When buying tulip bulbs, always look for guaranteed virus-free stock.

Note: Nerines can be disappointing for the first couple of years after planting, but should be left undisturbed. Once established as dense clumps, they will reward you annually with their vivid pink flowers produced at what can otherwise be a dull time of year.

To deter squirrels and other small rodents from digging up the bulbs, cover the planting area with a length of chicken wire.

Planting tulip bulbs

215

Gardening Under Cover

While you will want to make the most of any mild weather by spending as much time as possible outdoors, there are still some important jobs to do inside.

The Greenhouse

You will probably be emptying a lot of pots in which you have grown summer-fruiting vegetables and other plants. All spent compost can be added to the compost heap or simply thrown on bare earth in the garden, where it will benefit soil texture. Wash out all the pots, then stack them either under the greenhouse staging or in a shed or greenhouse. Take the opportunity now to give the greenhouse a thorough clean:

▶ **Shading:** Take down all blinds and netting used as shading during the previous months and wash them before storing for next year.

▶ **Tidy up:** Clear away all dead and dying foliage and flowers that might harbour disease.

216

▶ **Glass:** Clean the glass inside and out with a disinfectant. Pay particular attention to overlapping panes of glass – algae can grow where they touch.

▶ **Framework:** Scrub down the framework and all the staging.

▶ **Floor:** Sweep the floor and wash down with a disinfectant.

Note: Plastic plant pots normally can't go into the recycling bin, as they are already made from recycled material. Some garden centres and nurseries will accept them for reuse.

Top Tip

If you are heating the greenhouse over winter for the benefit of just a few plants, you can save on heating costs by grouping all the plants together at one end. Close this section off with a curtain of bubble plastic and heat this insulated area only.

Insulation

If you are planning on using the greenhouse over winter – even if only for storing plants in containers – insulate it against the worst of the coming cold weather. Stretch insulating material (such as heavy-duty bubble plastic) across the roof, holding it in position with adhesive tape. You may be able to use the same fixings from the summer shading material. You can also insulate the panes to the sides of the greenhouse, though you may lose some light in doing so.

Grapes

Prune grape vines now. Shorten the main stem or stems to keep them within bounds. Remove older, unproductive branches entirely, and tie in suitably placed stems as replacements. Shorten side shoots (which have produced the fruit) back to one bud from the base of each.

The Kitchen Garden

Now is the time to plan a fruit garden, as many fruit trees and bushes are available cheaply now, sold as bare-root plants.

Garlic

For successful cropping, garlic needs a period of cold. Planting during the coming weeks ensures the requisite number of hours at low temperatures. Garlic should be grown in well-prepared soil in a sunny, sheltered spot in the garden.

Top Tip

For the best results, look for specially produced garlic bulbs in garden centres and nurseries. Although you can use garlic from the supermarket, growth may not be as good.

▷ Snap each garlic bulb into its component cloves.

▷ With a dibber, make a row of holes in the soil about 10 cm (4 in) apart.

▷ Place one clove in each hole, then draw the surrounding soil over to cover. The tip of each clove should be just below the soil surface.

Apples

Pick late-fruiting varieties, either for immediate use or for storing. Plant new stock (*see* 'Bare-root Plants', p. 182).

Top Tip

When choosing an apple tree, look for an unusual variety, not the ones that are widely available in supermarkets. These have been bred to have a long shelf-life after picking. Ask your nearest fruit tree nursery which ones will do best in your locality.

Apple Canker

Apple canker – a serious disease – is first noticeable in autumn as a swelling of the bark, often at the site of a pruning wound or damaged bud. The central part of the swelling begins to die back and the bark flakes off, leaving a sunken discoloured area. Diseased patches should be cut back to healthy wood, using a knife or chisel. Burn the diseased material. The exposed healthy wood can be painted with a canker paint.

Soft Fruit

From now until late winter, bare-root fruit bushes will be available, often in multiples of five or more. This is the best time to buy and plant raspberries, gooseberries and all currants.

219

Planting Fruit Bushes

Fruit bushes are normally grown in rows or groups of one variety, but you can also grow a mix of two or more that will flower and fruit at slightly different times.

▶ **Soil:** Prepare the ground well beforehand, removing all large stones and perennial weeds and forking in organic matter or a soil improver.

▶ **Plant:** Dig planting holes large enough to accommodate the roots, paying attention to the recommended planting distances for each variety. Plant too far apart and pollination may be affected; too close and the plants will be vulnerable to fungal diseases (see also 'Bare-root Plants', p.182).

Note: Newly planted fruit bushes will not normally flower and fruit until the second year after planting.

Pruning Fruit Bushes

Most fruit bushes can be pruned now, or later during the dormant season, as follows:

▶ **New plantings:** To ensure strong new growth next year, shorten all stems by around a half.

▶ **Established bushes:** Shorten the current season's stems. Very vigorous growth can be left unpruned. Remove all older, unproductive stems entirely. The aim is to create a balanced framework of healthy stems with an open centre.

Top Tip

If you are growing a number of fruit bushes, it is worth investing in a fruit cage to protect the crops from birds (which will peck at the flowers and leaf buds, as well as any fruits that subsequently develop).

Note: Raspberries are pruned just after fruiting (summer varieties) or in early spring (autumn varieties).

Top Tip

If a bay tree in a container forms part of your herb garden, you can protect the roots over winter by digging a hole in a spare part of the garden and sinking the container into it.

Herbs

It's possible to keep some herbs going for a few weeks longer. Dig up clumps of mint, chives and marjoram, and pot them up. In an unheated greenhouse – or even in the kitchen – they will continue to provide fresh leaves for cooking.

Chives

Plants To Enjoy

Trees

Acer (maple)

Amelanchier

Arbutus (strawberry tree)

Betula (birch)

Cedrus atlantica 'Glauca' (blue
   Atlas cedar)

Cornus kousa

Ginkgo

Malus (crab apple)

Trachycarpus (Chusan palm)

Shrubs

Aucuba japonica

Berberis

Callicarpa

Calluna (heather)

Chaenomeles (ornamental
   quince, japonica)

Chusquea culeou (Chilean bamboo)

Cornus

Cotoneaster

Daboecia (heath)

Elaeagnus x ebbingei

Erica (heath)

Euonymus fortunei

x Fatshedera

Hamamelis (witch hazel)

Hebe

Ilex (holly)

Leucothöe

Lonicera (honeysuckle)

Pernettya

Phyllostachys nigra (black bamboo)

Pittosporum

Pyracantha (firethorn)

Nandina (heavenly bamboo)

Rubus thibetanus

Skimmia

Viburnum

Vinca (periwinkle)

Climbers

Hedera (ivy)

Jasminum nudiflorum
   (winter jasmine)

Aster (Michaelmas daisy)

Perennials

Artemisia

Cortaderia (pampas grass)

Aster (Michaelmas daisy)

Gentiana (gentian)

Hakonechloa

Helenium

Grasses

Ophiopogon planiscapus
   'Nigrescens'

Pennisetum

Phormium (New Zealand flax)

Schizostylis

Spartina

Stipa gigantean (golden oats)

Bulbs

Cyclamen

Checklist

▶ **Mulch for winter:** Apply a mulch of organic matter, ideally garden compost, around plants.

▶ **Trees and shrubs in containers:** Protect permanent woody plants from the worst frosts by wrapping the container in a length of fleece or an old blanket. Keep camellias well watered.

▶ **Evergreen shrubs:** This is the best time of year for moving established evergreens.

▶ **Conifers:** Move established and plant root-balled conifers on damp days when they will be least susceptible to 'transplant shock'.

▶ **Roses:** Lightly prune top-heavy roses that may be vulnerable to 'wind rock' in exposed gardens.

▶ **Climbers:** Tidy up wayward stems that grew late in the season.

▶ **Perennials:** Cover plants of borderline hardiness with a mulch of dry straw. Collect and sow seeds from perennials and grasses to build up stocks.

▶ **Bedding plants:** Plant hardy, early-flowering plants for flowers in the winter–spring period.

▶ **Greenhouses:** Clean the interior of the house while it is not in use. If it is to be used, insulate.

▶ **Garlic:** Plant garlic cloves, which need a period of cold to produce large heads.

▶ **Apples:** Check the bark of trees for signs of apple canker and treat accordingly.

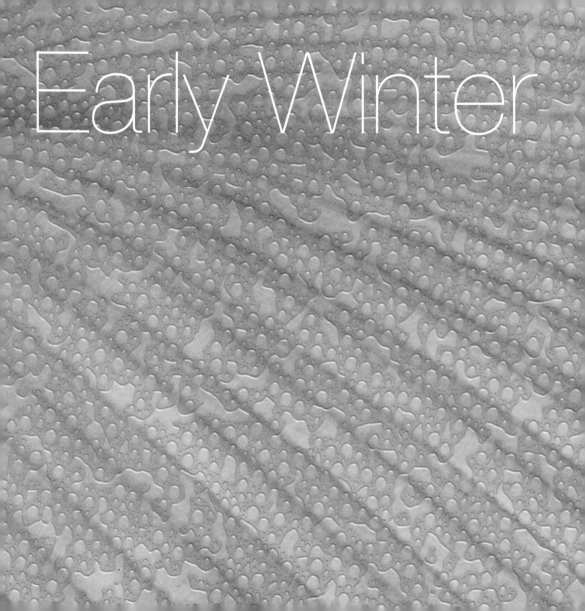

Early Winter

The Flower Garden

With the shortest day approaching, this is a quiet time in the garden. But you will spot a few flowers on winter-flowering shrubs on the odd sunny day.

Hardwood Cuttings

If you didn't get round to taking cuttings earlier in the year, it's not too late to try some now. By this time of year, growth is fully ripe and firm, so cuttings are classified as 'hardwood'. Rooting can be slow, however – taking six months to a year – but little aftercare is needed.

▶ **Trench:** With a spade, dig a narrow trench in the soil about 20 cm (8 in) deep – it is usually sufficient just to push in the spade and rock it to and fro.

▶ **Sand:** Line the base of the trench with a 2.5 cm (1 in) layer of grit or sharp sand.

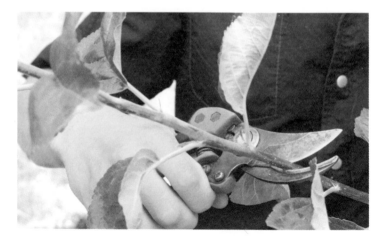

▶ **Cuttings:** Take cuttings up to 30 cm (12 in) long from the plant, each of which should have four or more buds (leaf joints) or pairs of buds. Trim each cutting at the base, just below a bud (or pair), and at the tip, just above a bud (or pair).

▶ **Plant:** Insert the cuttings into the trench so that the uppermost buds protrude above ground level.

▶ **Aftercare:** Firm in the cuttings, label them and water them in well.

▶ **Position:** By the following autumn (sometimes earlier), the cuttings should be well rooted and can be moved to their final positions.

Note: Hardwood cuttings of evergreen plants should be treated as semi-ripe cuttings (see p. 184) and rooted in containers in a cold frame.

Hormone Rooting Compounds

The jury is out on hormone rooting compounds – powders or liquids that are applied to the trimmed base of a cutting. While they are supposed to speed up rooting, most cuttings will root successfully without them. However, a dab of compound can be beneficial for hardwood cuttings that can otherwise show some reluctance. Even so, its use is not strictly necessary.

Gardening Under Cover

There is not so much to do at this time of year, except to make sure that overwintering plants have good light, are not too cold and do not dry out excessively.

The Greenhouse

On mild days, open all the vents and the door to maintain good air circulation. But be aware that some measure of pest control may still be necessary.

Protecting Stored Items

Mice will eat bulbs, fruits and vegetables in storage. They do not actually hibernate, but enter a state of torpor during cold spells. In milder weather – when you may be ventilating places where plant material is being stored – they will be looking for food. Either put down poisoned bait or set traps. Some of these trap the animals live, allowing you to return them to the wild, some distance from the garden.

If you are storing summer bulbs, such as dahlias, gladioli and begonias, check them over periodically. Throw away any that have softened and are showing signs of rot. Dust the remainder with a fungicidal powder to keep them healthy.

Cold Frames

Cold frames – sometimes made of glass or, more usually these days, a sturdy
synthetic material – will protect plants from strong winds, heavy rain and light frost.

However, any plants inside will still be vulnerable to prolonged freezing temperatures. On really cold
nights, insulate the frame by laying a piece of old carpet or a thick blanket on the top. This can be
removed during daylight hours, though it is best left in place if the temperature remains below freezing.

On mild days, keep the frame open to maintain good air flow. Some fungal diseases can proliferate even
at low temperatures, so stagnant air should not be allowed to build up in the frame.

The Kitchen Garden

You may still be lifting root vegetables, but this time of year also gives you a good opportunity for forward planning. Dig over all vacant beds to prepare for next season.

Apples and Pears

As they enter their period of dormancy, these fruit trees can be pruned. Thin older branches to open up the crown and cut back damaged ones entirely. Cut back diseased growth and burn the prunings. However, do not prune too hard or you will encourage a mass of thin, sappy stems to grow next spring that will not crop well.

Plants To Enjoy

Trees

Arbutus (strawberry tree)

Betula (birch)

Prunus serrula

Shrubs

Callicarpa

Chimonanthus praecox (wintersweet)

Cornus

Erica (heather)

Hamemelis mollis (witch hazel)

Ilex (holly)

Mahonia

Skimmia

Viburnum

Climbers

Clematis cirrhosa

Jasminum nudiflorum
  (winter jasmine)

Perennials

Iris unguicularis

Helleborus niger
  (Christmas rose)

Bulbs

Cyclamen

Annuals and biennials

Viola, Wittrockiana Group (pansy)

Checklist

▶ **Cuttings:** Take hardwood cuttings of a range of plants. Root them either in a trench dug outdoors or in pots that can be kept in a cold frame or unheated greenhouse.

▶ **Greenhouses:** Ventilate the house on mild days by opening the door and all vents.

▶ **Mice:** Set traps for mice in enclosed areas that are being used to store fruits, vegetables and bulbs. The pests will be active during mild spells when you may be looking to ventilate these areas.

▶ **Cold frames:** Insulate frames during periods of cold weather by placing a small piece of carpet over the lid. Remove this when the weather turns mild and leave the lid open.

▶ **Prepare ground for next year:** Bare plots in the vegetable garden can be improved by digging in organic matter such as garden compost, soil improver or well-rotted farmyard manure. Alternatively, simply spread the material on the soil surface and allow it to be incorporated naturally.

▶ **Root vegetables:** Dig up root vegetables left in the ground for immediate use.

▶ **Brussels sprouts:** For the sweetest flavour, pick the sprouts after the first hard frost.

▶ **Apples and pears:** Prune apple and pear trees. Shred or burn the prunings (all material showing signs of disease is best burnt).

Mid-Winter

The Flower Garden

Despite the dark, you can take comfort in the fact that spring really is only just around the corner. The shortest day marks the end of the rest period for many plants.

Root Cuttings

These are an excellent way of increasing stocks of a number of hardy perennials, and it is best done now, when the plants are dormant. Prepare 12.5 cm (5 in) pots of potting compost mixed with grit or sharp sand.

▶ **Clean:** Dig up established plants and wash the roots free of soil.

▶ **Choose:** Cut off healthy, thicker roots close to the crown. Replant the parent plant.

▶ **Section:** Cut the roots into 5 cm (2 in) lengths. Angle the cut at the base of each so that you can tell which is the correct way up.

▶ **Compost:** Make holes in the compost with a dibber or pencil and insert the cuttings with the straight uppermost cut level with the compost surface.

▶ **Position:** Label the cuttings and put them in a cold frame or unheated greenhouse.

▶ **Aftercare:** New growth should appear in spring. In late spring or early summer, the cuttings can be potted up individually.

Plants Suitable for Root Cuttings

Acanthus (bear's breeches)

Anemone x japonica

Echinops ritro

Gaillarda

Papaver orientale (poppy)

Phlox maculata

Phlox paniculata

Pulsatilla vulgaris (Pasque flower)

Romneya coulteri (California poppy)

Papaver orientale (poppy)

Note: For plants with thin roots, such as phlox and anemone, cut thin lengths of root and lay them on trays of potting compost mixed with grit or sharp sand. Top with a layer of sand.

Bonfires

Many gardeners love a good bonfire at this time of year, and it's an excellent way to get rid of a whole lot of material that's unsuitable for composting. But check with your local authority whether there are any restrictions. If you have built up a pile over a series of weeks, turn it over gently with a garden fork before lighting it. Hedgehogs and other small mammals may be using it as a winter nest and need time to relocate.

235

Gardening Under Cover

This is a quiet time of year for indoor plants, so your priority is to keep them ticking over. They will soon spring back into life when there is more daylight available.

Storage

Check over all bulbs, fruits and vegetables in storage. Continue to set traps for mice (see p. 228) if you spot any signs of damage.

Houseplants

Keep houseplants in a light position but out of draughts. Pick off and burn dead leaves. Water cacti if they appear to be shrivelling – otherwise, keep them dry.

Hippeastrums

Amaryllis bulbs – more correctly *Hippeastrum* – are often seen on sale at this time of year, and they make attractive plants for indoors. Plant the bulbs with the top half above the compost surface. If growth is a little slow, put them somewhere warm. Insert a cane next to the bulb on planting to support the stem.

The Kitchen Garden

Time now is mainly given over to planning the productive garden – not even weeds are germinating during the dark days. This is an excellent time for improving ground that's seen heavy use over the year.

Liming

Some gardeners add lime to the vegetable plot at this time of year, as it can increase yields. Do not add lime and farmyard manure at the same time, however – the two react together and release ammonia. Add the lime as far in advance of planting as you can. Apply it during a period of still weather so that it does not blow away. Wear gloves and goggles, as lime is caustic.

Rhubarb

For early, sweet-flavoured stems, cover the crowns with a large bucket or special rhubarb forcer. Excluding light encourages early growth that is pale, thin and tender.

Note: Forcing weakens rhubarb, so plants given this treatment should be allowed to grow normally the next year. If you have several, you can alternate.

Did You Know?

Rhubarb is not a fruit but a vegetable, as it's the stems that are eaten. Once the flowers appear, the stems are inedible.

Plants To Enjoy

Shrubs

Chimonanthus praecox
   (wintersweet)
Cornus
Daphne mezereum
Garrya elliptica
Hamamelis (witch hazel)
Ilex (holly)

Lonicera fragrantissima
Mahonia x media
Skimmia
Viburnum

Climbers

Jasminum nudiflorum
   (winter jasmine)

Jasminum nudiflorum (winter jasmine)

Perennials

Helleborus niger
   (Christmas rose)

Bulbs

Crocus
Eranthis (winter aconite)
Galanthus (snowdrop)

Annuals and biennials

Viola, Wittrockiana Group
   (pansy)

Mahonia x media

238

Checklist

▶ **Cuttings·** Perennials: Increase your stocks of a number of plants by taking root cuttings now, while the plants are fully dormant.

▶ **Bonfires:** Get rid of all woody prunings and diseased plant remains by setting fire to them. Add the ashes to the compost heap when cool, or use them as an organic source of potassium for feeding fruit trees and roses and other flowering shrubs. Fires should be lit only during still weather and must be supervised at all times.

▶ **Houseplants:** Keep all houseplants in as light a position as possible at this time of year. Move them away from windows (unless insulated) on very cold nights, as they may suffer from the sudden drop in temperature.

▶ **Cacti:** Keep cacti dry during the winter, as they should have sufficient water stored in their swollen bodies. Water them only if they appear to be shrivelling.

▶ **Amaryllis:** Plant up amaryllis bulbs for growing indoors during the winter months.

▶ **Liming:** Add lime to bare soil in the vegetable garden – but not if you have recently added manure.

▶ **Rhubarb:** Force rhubarb plants to produce quantities of fresh pink stems by excluding light from the plants. If you don't have a special rhubarb forcer, use an upturned waste bin.

▶ **Storage:** Continue to keep an eye on bulbs, fruits and vegetables in storage and protect from pests.

Late-Winter

The Flower Garden

This is usually the coldest time of year, but it can also be an exciting time in the garden, when the spring bulbs start to show and there are new buds on shrubs and trees.

Shrubs and Climbers

As their natural period of dormancy is coming to an end, this is an ideal time for taking action on many plants that have been allowed to get out of hand.

Renewal Pruning

Neglected, overgrown shrubs and climbers can be given a new lease of life by hard pruning – drastic, but generally supremely effective. Cut back all stems to within 15–30 cm (6–12 in) of the ground. A rather more cautious approach is to cut back only one half to a third of the stems. If recovery is good, cut back the remainder the same time next year.

Wisteria

Although the main pruning of wisteria is done in late summer, for the best flowering you can shorten side shoots now. This will result in fewer but larger flowers. Cut them back to 8–10 cm (3–4 in) – each pruned shoot should have only two or three buds on it.

Clematis

Group 3 clematis, which flower from summer onwards, can be pruned hard now (see p. 91). Shorten all stems to 15–30 cm (6–12 in) of the ground.

Perennials

If you did not do so in autumn, cut back any dead growth on perennials to allow new growth to develop. Groom grasses by pulling or cutting out all the dead leaves.

Dividing Snowdrops

Dig up and divide snowdrops that have flowered. Use a fork to lift established clumps while they are still in leaf. Separate out the bulbs and then replant them in groups of five or more.

Planting 'in the Green'

Unlike most other bulbs, snowdrops (Galanthus) and winter aconites (Eranthis hyemalis) do not do well if planted as bare bulbs in autumn. It is best to buy them now, as leafy plants that have just finished flowering. After planting, the leaves often collapse, but this is natural – they are simply starting to die back. The bulbs will flower normally next year.

'Blind' Bulbs

Established clumps of bulbs sometimes fail to flower, producing a mass of leaves instead. This is because the bulbs are too congested underground and cannot expand to flowering size. Fork up the clumps and separate out the individual bulbs. Replant them with sufficient space between each so that they will fill out and flower the following year

Gardening Under Cover

Keen gardeners will want to make good use of the increase in natural light. You can bring overwintered plants back into commission and also start seed sowing.

Fuchsias

If you have overwintered fuchsias in a cool, dry place, stimulate new growth by putting them in full light in slightly warmer conditions. Begin watering and mist the stems to encourage bud break. If a plant is very old and woody, you can use any new stems that are produced as softwood cuttings (see p. 99).

Pelargoniums

Start watering pelargoniums more regularly. In a heated greenhouse or conservatory, some may even start to flower.

Sweet Peas

If you didn't manage to sow sweet peas the previous autumn, sow seeds now, in an unheated greenhouse or cold frame. Use 12.5 cm (5 in) pots filled with seed or multi-purpose compost. Stand the seedlings outdoors on mild days – too much warmth at this stage will lead to straggly growth.

The Kitchen Garden

Keep off the soil if the ground is frozen or waterlogged but, if not, continue to dig it over, adding garden compost, well-rotted farmyard manure or soil improver.

Preparing the Soil

If you want to make some early sowings, you can warm up areas of soil by placing tunnel cloches over the surface. To warm up a larger area, spread a length of black plastic or horticultural fleece over the ground, held in position with large stones or bricks.

Deterring Birds

Birds are generally welcome in a garden, as they feed on slugs and insect pests. But they can also be pests themselves, as they will peck at the emerging green buds on fruit trees.

If you don't have a fruit cage to keep them out, hang old CDs and foil pans from the branches of trees so that they spin in the breeze and catch the light, thus deterring the birds. Netting fruit trees individually is not recommended because the birds can become trapped in the mesh.

245

Plants To Enjoy

Shrubs

Chimonanthus praecox
(winter sweet)

Cornus

Daphne mezereum

Garrya elliptica

Hamamelis (witch hazel)

Lonicera fragrantissima

Mahonia

Pyracantha (firethorn)

Skimmia

Iris reticulata

Eranthis (winter aconite)

Climbers

Jasminum nudiflorum
(winter jasmine)

Perennials

Helleborus niger
(Christmas rose)

Bulbs

Chionodoxa
(glory of the snow)

Crocus

Eranthis
(winter aconite)

Galanthus (snowdrop)

Iris reticulata

Muscari
(grape hyacinth)

Annuals and biennials

Viola, Wittrockiana Group
(pansy)

Checklist

▶ **Shrubs and climbers:** Prune hard any overgrown or neglected shrubs and climbers.

▶ **Wisteria:** Shorten side shoots on the main stems now to produce the most spectacular flowering display.

▶ **Clematis:** Prune Group 3 clematis back to 15–30 cm (6–12 in) of ground level.

▶ **Perennials:** If you did not do so in autumn, cut back any old dead growth on perennials to allow room for the new.

▶ **Grasses:** Cut out all old leaves and flower stems left on the plants over winter.

▶ **Snowdrops:** Dig up and divide congested clumps. Also make new plantings of snowdrops 'in the green'.

▶ **Fuchsias:** Bring overwintered fuchsias back into growth by increasing the heat and light levels and watering the compost. Spray woody stems with water to encourage them to break.

▶ **Sweet peas:** Sow seed now if you did not do so the previous autumn.

▶ **Vegetables:** Warm the ground for early sowings, and for planting early potatoes, by covering the planting area with a cloche or length of horticultural fleece or heavy-duty black plastic.

▶ **Birds:** Keep birds away from fruit trees and fruit bushes, as they will peck at the emerging leaf and flower buds in their search for food. Put out food and water for them elsewhere in the garden.

Calendar of Care

Early Spring
The Flower Garden
- [ ] Improve the soil by adding garden compost or other improver.
- [ ] Start mowing lawns.
- [ ] Make new lawns.
- [ ] Divide congested clumps of early bulbs that have already flowered.
- [ ] Plant out sweet pea seedlings.
- [ ] Prune roses.

Gardening Under Cover
- [ ] Start regular watering and feeding of houseplants.

The Kitchen Garden
- [ ] Sow seed of vegetables that need a long growing season.
- [ ] Plant onion sets.
- [ ] Hand pollinate peach and other fruit trees.

Mid-Spring
The Flower Garden
- [ ] Make new lawns.
- [ ] Plant evergreen trees and shrubs for hedging.
- [ ] Stake perennials as required.
- [ ] Dead-head early bulbs that have finished flowering.
- [ ] Start dahlia tubers into growth.
- [ ] Plant new lily bulbs.

Gardening Under Cover
- [ ] Sow seeds of tender vegetables.

The Kitchen Garden
- [ ] Sow vegetable seeds in their cropping positions.
- [ ] Protect seedling crops from birds and insect pests.
- [ ] Plant potatoes or start them into growth indoors.

Late Spring
The Flower Garden
- [ ] Prune shrubs that have finished flowering.
- [ ] Treat roses for greenfly, if necessary.
- [ ] Train in new stems on climbers.
- [ ] Clip or shear hedges.
- [ ] Plant up hanging baskets ready for summer.
- [ ] Treat weeds with a weedkiller.
- [ ] Treat all timber – decking, fence panels and sheds – in the garden with a wood preservative.

Gardening Under Cover
- [ ] Sow seeds of half-hardy annuals ready for planting out in summer.

The Kitchen Garden

- Spray apples and pears in flower, as appropriate.

Early Summer
The Flower Garden

- Remove suckers from around the bases of trees and shrubs.
- Prune plum trees and other members of the *Prunus* genus, including ornamentals.
- Take softwood cuttings of shrubs.
- Remove the faded flowers or cut back to ground level perennials that have already flowered.
- Plant out bedding plants.

Gardening Under Cover

- Tie in the stems on cordon tomatoes.
- Ventilate greenhouses during hot weather.

The Kitchen Garden

- Plant outdoor tomatoes.
- Thin seedlings of crops sown in rows.
- Protect fruits on strawberry plants.

Mid-Summer
The Flower Garden

- Water lawns or leave them unmown during periods of drought.
- Dead-head repeat-flowering roses.
- Divide irises with thick rhizomes.
- Plant autumn-flowering bulbs.
- Top up the pond if the water level drops.

Gardening Under Cover

- Shade greenhouses by applying a wash to the glass or fixing shading fabric in place.
- Turn plants regularly to maintain even growth.

The Kitchen Garden

- Water vegetable plants regularly.
- Harvest early potatoes.
- Pick the leaves of cut-and-come-again crops and sow seeds for replacements later.

Late Summer
The Flower Garden

- Give hedges their second cut of the season.
- Tie in new stems on all climbing plants.
- Take cuttings of shrubs and climbers.
- Control earwigs that may be damaging flowers.

Gardening Under Cover

- Bring dormant tubers of cyclamen back into growth.
- Check plants in pots for signs of vine weevil damage.

The Kitchen Garden

- Harvest onions.
- Make late sowings of salad crops.
- Pick plums, cherries and peaches.

Early Autumn
The Flower Garden

- Rake, spike and top-dress lawns.
- Eliminate moss on lawns with a moss-killer.
- Plant spring bulbs.
- Make sowings of hardy annuals for early flowers next year.

Gardening Under Cover

- Remove shading from greenhouses and wipe off shading washes.

The Kitchen Garden

- To fill bare soil, replace harvested vegetables with green manure plants.
- Lift beetroots, carrots and other root vegetables.
- Ripen green tomatoes by laying stems on the ground.
- Harvest ripe apples and pears.
- Plant new strawberry plants.
- Cut back fruited canes on blackberries and related plants.

Mid-Autumn
The Flower Garden

- Make leaf mould from fallen leaves.
- Plant bare-root trees and shrubs or heel them in for planting later.
- Take cuttings of shrubs and climbers.
- Cut back and divide overgrown perennials.
- Lift dahlia tubers and dry them off for storing over winter.
- Plant spring bulbs.
- Put protective covers around tree ferns (*Dicksonia*) and other plants that are not fully hardy.
- Sow sweet pea seeds.

Gardening Under Cover

- Pot up bulbs for growing in unheated greenhouses.
- Plant forced bulbs for indoor flowers in winter.

The Kitchen Garden

- Dig up and dry off maincrop potatoes for storing.
- Pick later-ripening apples.
- Cut back fruited stems on summer-fruiting raspberries.

Late Autumn
The Flower Garden

- Spread a mulch around plants and over beds and borders.
- Regularly water camellias in containers.
- For protection from hard frosts, wrap a protective fabric around containers planted with permanent shrubs and trees.
- Move established evergreens and conifers, if necessary.
- Plant root-balled conifers.
- Prune roses to prevent 'wind rock', if necessary.

- [ ] Tidy up wayward stems on climbers.
- [ ] Plant bedding plants for late-winter interest.

Gardening Under Cover

- [ ] Clean the interiors of greenhouses.
- [ ] Insulate greenhouses with suitable materials.

The Kitchen Garden

- [ ] Plant garlic.
- [ ] Check the bark of apple trees and other fruit trees for signs of canker.

Early Winter
The Flower Garden

- [ ] Take hardwood cuttings of trees and shrubs.

Gardening Under Cover

- [ ] Ventilate greenhouses and cold frames on mild days.
- [ ] Insulate cold frames during very cold periods.
- [ ] Set traps for mice in sheds, garages and outbuildings where fruits and vegetables are stored.

The Kitchen Garden

- [ ] Harvest root vegetables.
- [ ] Harvest Brussels sprouts.
- [ ] Prune apple and pear trees.

Mid-Winter
The Flower Garden

- [ ] Take root cuttings of certain perennials.

Gardening Under Cover

- [ ] Move all houseplants into a light position.
- [ ] Water cacti if they appear shrivelled.
- [ ] Pot up amaryllis (*Hippeastrum*) bulbs.

The Kitchen Garden

- [ ] Lime the soil, if necessary.
- [ ] Force established rhubarb plants for early stems.

Late Winter
The Flower Garden

- [ ] Prune overgrown, neglected or congested shrubs and climbers.
- [ ] Prune Group 3 clematis.
- [ ] Cut back overwintered dead growth on perennials and grasses.
- [ ] Dig up and divide congested clumps of snowdrops (*Galanthus*).

Gardening Under Cover

- [ ] Bring overwintered fuchsias back into growth.

The Kitchen Garden

- [ ] Warm up the soil for early sowings and for planting potatoes.
- [ ] Keep birds away from fruit trees and shrubs.

251

Further Reading
& Websites

Bradley, S., *A Year in the Garden: A Step-by-step Guide to Vital Gardening Projects Through the Year*, Ryland, Peters & Small Ltd., 2009

Diacono, M., *Fruit (River Cottage Handbook)*, Bloomsbury Publishing PLC, 2011

Evelegh, T., *Gardening in No Time: 50 Step-By-Step Projects and Inspirational Ideas*, Cico, 2011

Harrison, J., *Vegetable Growing Month-by-Month: The Down-To-Earth Guide That Takes You Through The Vegetable Year*, Right Way, 2008

Hashman, J., *Pocket Guide to the Edible Garden: What To Do And When, Month By Month*, Spring Hill, 2010

Hessayon, Dr D.G., *The Green Garden Expert*, Expert, 2009

Joyce, D., *The Best Flowers to Grow and Cut*, Frances Lincoln, 2004

Step Mikolajski, A., *Hanging Baskets: Create Stunning Seasonal Displays for Your Garden*, Southwater, 2002

Reader's Digest, *Food from Your Garden and Allotment*, Reader's Digest, 2008

Royal Horticultural, *RHS Encyclopedia of Garden Design*, Dorling Kindersley, 2009

Strauss, R., *Grow Your Own Vegetables: How to Grow, What to Grow, When to Grow*, Flame Tree Publishing, 2010

Titchmarsh, A., *The Gardener's Year*, BBC Books, 2005

Whittingham, J., *Grow Something to Eat Every Day*, Dorling Kindersley, 2011

www.bbc.co.uk/gardening/digin
BBC site which gives advice on how to grow and then cook your own food, using accessible video tutorials to accompany text.

www.garden.org
The website for the United States' National Gardening Association. It has an extensive range of content, from 'How-To' videos to details of community seed swaps.

www.gardenorganic.org.uk
The website of this national charity aimed at promoting organic growing offers news about gardening events, access to their catalogue and information about display gardens across the UK.

www.gardenweb.com
Hosts a number of blogs and forums, as well as articles on gardening and an 'Ask the Experts' section.

www.growsonyou.com/gardening/front-garden-ideas
Offers imaginative ideas about and photos of well-designed front gardens.

www.lewisgardens.com/beginner.htm
This site offers detailed help for gardening beginners, as well as selling pre-planned garden flower layouts.

www.lovethegarden.com
This informative website offers wide-ranging gardening advice about flower, house, vegetable and lawn cultivation as well as gardening product information, forums and advice on dealing with pests.

www.rhs.org.uk/Gardening
The Royal Horticultural Society site offers extensive gardening advice and even has a 'gardener's calendar'. It also has a forum.

www.suttons.co.uk
Award-winning retailer of seeds and garden equipment.

www.urbangardensweb.com
This website presents innovative and eco-friendly garden designs for city dwellers who are short of garden space.

Index